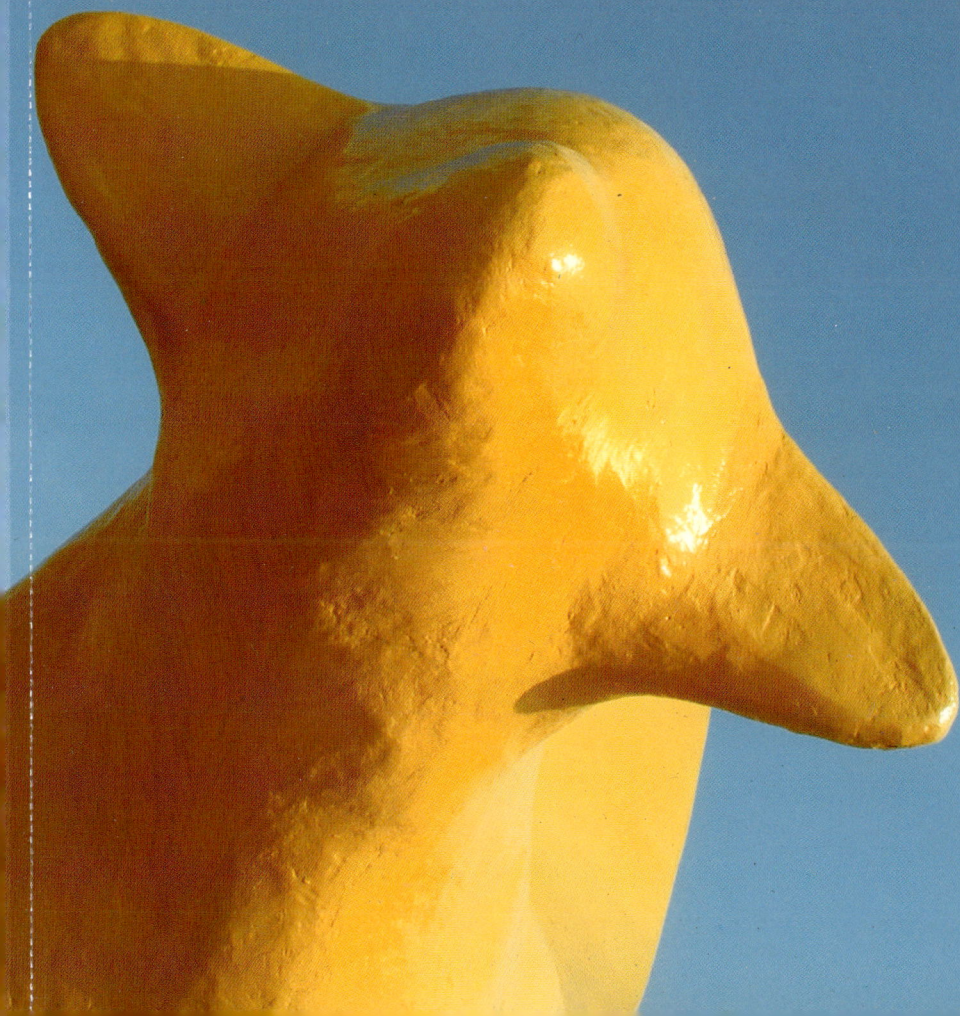

LIVERPOOL
THE GUIDE 2005/06

SuperLambBanana. The world in one city. The city in one book. Order online at: **www.liverpooltheguide.com**

LIVERPOOL
THE GUIDE 2005/06

Second Edition

Contents

The city in one book...

■ Liverpool is back – and so is this definitive annual guidebook. One year on from our inaugural edition comes a fully revised version for 2005/06, bringing you bang up-to-date as the forthcoming European Capital of Culture continues its renaissance. Inside you'll find all the info you need about the latest tourist attractions, the new bars, clubs and restaurants, the fashion and shopping and best places to stay – as well as unbeatable coverage of Liverpool's nightlife, arts, culture, entertainment and sport. Lots of maps, too, plus six very walkable districts to explore, and a comprehensive directory with every address, phone number and website you'll need. Whether you're Liverpool born-and-bred or one of its two million annual visitors, we like to think you're holding the only guide that gets to the heart and soul of a city reborn, exciting and inspiring. The real deal, written and produced by native Liverpudlians who know the score. Enjoy...

Editor
■ David Cottrell
Art and Design
■ Christopher Abram
Product Manager
■ Cathryn O'Grady
Product Development
■ Jane Johnson
Sponsorship Manager
■ Laura Churchill
Advertising Sales
■ Mike Brear

Thanks to...
■ Gillian Guilfoyle, Katherine Percival, Katherine Carlisle, Felicity Ovie, Zuhra Herwitker, Steven Pattison, Stephanie Jones, Tracy Smith and Ruth Hobbins (Central Library). Images of old Liverpool courtesy of the Project P.O.O.L. CD-Rom available from the Record Office, 4th Floor Central Library, priced £15.

The publishers and authors have done their best to ensure the accuracy and currency of all the information in Liverpool: The Guide 2005/06. However, they can accept no responsibility for any loss, injury or inconvenience sustained as a result of information or advice contained in this guide.

■ A Soft Joe Production.
Published by:
Trinity Mirror Merseyside

a **Trinity Mirror** business

Distribution:
Orca Booksellers.
Printers:
The Journal Printing Company Limited.

Liverpool is...

Not really north. Not quite Midlands. Closer to Wales and Ireland. And definitely Atlantic. Or is it just a state of mind?

Changing...

■ You can't help but notice the Big Dig – the massive transformation of Liverpool to the tune of £3billion, including the Paradise Project (biggest retail scheme of its kind in Europe), King's Waterfront (major arena and conference zone), forthcoming Merseytram system and cruise-liner facility, and City Centre Movement Strategy (improving access all over town). Mind the gap.

Connected...

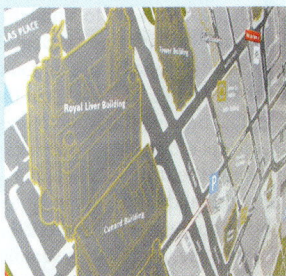

■ Easy to reach and pretty effortless to explore, with two handy tourist centres and plenty of signs and information panels to keep you, er, informed and on the right track. There's a big screen, too, at Clayton Square, and a very visible campaign to keep locals and visitors aware of all the current transformations taking place. If you still get lost, just ask one of the natives.

Lively...

■ Welcome to a vibrant city-centre with a growing population, whole raft of stylish and innovative new developments and lots of bright public spaces. The nightlife? In a word, legendary. The city celebrates its 800th birthday in 2007, and the following year it's officially the European Capital of Culture. One or two little shindigs being planned, we're led to believe.

Appetising...

■ Peckish? Choose from at least 50 restaurants within easy reach with a breadth and variety of cuisine worthy of a cosmopolitan, 21st Century city. There's British, French, Italian, Spanish, Portuguese, Indian, Chinese, Japanese, Thai, North American, Mexican, Chilean, Russian, Turkish and Greek. And that's not counting the cafés, bistros, gastropubs, lounge bars, hotels etc.

DAY TWO: Step right this way for a **Magical Mystery Tour** (tickets from Beatles Story, Queen Square Information Centre or 0151 709 3285) by coach to **Penny Lane,** where the barber still shaves another customer, and **Strawberry Field,** the former children's home where John used to play.

In the afternoon, take a scheduled tour to **Mendips and 20 Forthlin Road,** the childhood homes of John and Paul respectively and now run by the National Trust (for tickets call 0151 427 7231).

Back in town for a bite to eat at **The Pilgrim** on the street of the same name, popular with students from the Liverpool Institute of Performing Arts and adorned with art from Rubber Soul. Then head for **LIPA** itself on Hope Street – formerly the **Liverpool Insitute** attended by George and Paul (who has an auditorium named after him). Also here, the old **Liverpool School of Art** (now part of JMU) that numbered John and Stuart Sutcliffe among its students. The pair shared a flat at **no9 Percy Street,** near to Catharine Street.

Finish off with a well-deserved mini pub crawl. On Rice Street (off Hope Street) is **Ye Cracke** where John formed his first band the Dissenters over a pint or two in June 1960. Head downhill for a few minutes till you reach the **Blue Angel** on Seel Street, once run by Beatles agent Allan Williams and graced by the likes of Bob Dylan and Judy Garland.

Then it's late last orders at erstwhile beatnik haunt the **Jacaranda** (Slater Street). They found murals by John here when they scrubbed down the basement walls, and his ghost was allegedly seen arguing with a barmaid from 1959 called Audrey. He always was the bolshie one.

Stop press...
The **Yellow Submarine** has been temporarily removed from The Strand (opposite Albert Dock) while the Paradise Project is ongoing. Look out for a **Hard Day's Night Hotel** on North John Street (right by Mathew Street) in the coming months, and don't forget the **International Beatles Week** runs for six days in August every year.

Photogenic...

■ Liverpool looks good, which is why so many feature films and major TV dramas continue to be shot here. The city's Film Office organised the equivalent of 596 days of filming during 2004. Productions include the BBC's Casanova, an Elizabethan costume drama filmed at St George's Hall and Stanley Dock, and Alfie, starring Jude Law and featuring several scenes in which Liverpool doubled as New York.

Lyrical...

■ Music's been a way of life at least since the 'Cunard Yanks' – Liverpool seaman returning home from the States in the 1950s – brought back the jeans, guitars and rock 'n' roll records that spawned the Merseybeat sound. After an explosion of new bands in the 80s, Cream dominated the world of clubbing through to the turn of the century, and today Liverpool's streetwise live-music scene remains as exciting and diverse as ever.

Must see must do

Tourist ticklist. Two timescales. Take your pick...

■ **SHORT AND SWEET:** Take a dash through the new **Williamson Square fountain** – without getting your feet or head wet. Then have a swift one in the one and only **Cooper's,** a quintessential Scouse alehouse just outside Clayton Square shopping arcade.

and then – courtesy of the super-duper Creamselector touch-screen dispenser.

Take in a blockbuster or art-house movie in the second-floor cinemas at **FACT** – and sink into their luxurious, ergonomically-designed seats. And re-live those

■ ALL THE TIME IN THE WORLD:
Stay over in style at the **Radisson SAS hotel,** and admire its **Face of Liverpool** urban art project. Unleash your digital camera on all eight of Liverpool's **Grade I listed buildings** – Albert Dock, Royal Liver Building, Oriel Chambers, Town Hall, Bank of England, Bluecoat Chambers, St George's Hall and Anglican Cathedral.

Take an hour-long **Mersey Ferries River Explorer Cruise** (the Iris and Daffodil are 'Royal', by the way, because they saw action at Zeebrugge in the Great War).

Have a long, lazy lunch at the **Liverpool Marina & Harbourside Club,** serenaded by seagulls and the clink of forestays on masts.

Go modern at **Tate Liverpool** (Albert Dock) and native at the nearby **Museum of Liverpool Life.** Then shoot the breeze in **St John's Gardens** after you've perused the international collections in **World Museum Liverpool** and the **Walker.**

Experience the old Spion Kop on a tour of **Liverpool FC's Anfield stadium and club museum.**

Hunt the ghost – phantoms in the very old **Slaughterhouse** pub (Fenwick Street), lingering tobacco smoke at the **Cotton Exchange,** and the famous White Lady in the **Philharmonic Hall.**

Smash a few plates at Greek restaurant **Christakis,** or toast your good taste with the very best vodka at **St Petersburg** – both unforgettable, both on York Street (off Duke Street).

Lark about on **Lark Lane** then ramble through nearby – and quite glorious – **Sefton Park.**

Go on a **Hope Quarter pub crawl** – the Roscoe Head, Philharmonic, Blackburne Arms and Peter Kavanagh's, for starters.

Explore one of the most beautiful **synagogues** in Anglo-Jewry on Princes Road, then visit the splendid **Greek Church of St Nicholas** across the road.

Watch whatever's on at the born-again **Playhouse** or **Everyman** theatres – compelling drama and a great night-out guaranteed.

■ For all phone numbers and websites see **Details page 199.**

Historic...

■ Liverpool is a World Heritage city, inscribed by UNESCO thus: 'Six areas in the historic centre and docklands of the maritime mercantile City of Liverpool bear witness to the development of one of the world's major trading centres in the 18th and 19th Centuries. Liverpool played an important role in the growth of the British Empire and became the major port for the mass movement of people, e.g. slaves and emigrants from northern Europe to America. Liverpool was a pioneer in the development of modern dock technology, transport systems, and port management. The listed sites feature a great number of significant commercial, civic and public buildings, including St George's Plateau'.

Seeing stars

Where to spot a famous face...

■ **Victoria Street** – you'll have to look the part to get a glimpse of the soap stars, sportsmen and women, musicians and actors in town. Try the Living Room and its VIP Mosquito club, plus Metro, the Late Lounge and Marquee. Nearby Spanish restaurant La Vina is a hit with Liverpool FC's Spanish contingent, while the glitzy Newz Bar on Water Street is another favourite haunt. **Albert Dock** – stars pop in frequently at Baby Cream, Blue Bar & Grill and the Pan American Club, from visiting Premiership football teams to bone fide A-List Hollywood celebs. **Mathew Street** – more specifically fashion store Wade Smith, where a lot of the players from Liverpool and Everton FC get their threads. **Radisson SAS, Crowne Plaza Hotel, Hope Street Hotel and Racquet Club** – their respective bars and restaurants are all pretty good for glimpsing visiting pop stars and thespians relaxing after a gritty performance, but don't be too nosy.

And Liverpool's great and good from days gone by...

■ **John Brodie** (Mersey tunnel engineer) relief outside Queensway entrance; **William Brown** (philanthropist) statue in St George's Hall; **Dr William Duncan** (first Medical Officer) pub sign on St John's Lane; **George Canning** (politician) statue in Town Hall; **Dixie Dean** (Everton FC legend) statue at Goodison Park; **Billy Fury** (rocker, left) statue at Museum of Liverpool Life; **William Gladstone** (Prime Minister) statue in St John's Gardens; **William Huskisson** (politician) statue in St James Cemetery; **Agnes Jones** (nursing pioneer) statue in Oratory by Anglican Cathedral; **William Rathbone** (slavery abolitionist) statue in St George's Hall; **William Roscoe** (philanthropist) pub sign on Roscoe Street; **Bill Shankly** (Liverpool FC legend) statue at Anfield; **Kitty Wilkinson** (cholera heroine) stained glass in Anglican Cathedral.

Kids stuff

Keeping the children occupied is easy...

■ Pride of place among Liverpool's many attractions and activities for children is the all-new World Museum on William Brown Street. It opened in spring 2004 after a £35million expansion that's doubled its size and allowed thousands of fascinating artefacts to go on show for the first time in 50 years. The new wing is beautifully designed and fully interactive, with six floors, a theatre, café and lots of places to play and rest. Don't miss (as if you can) the dinosaurs, giant creepie-crawlies that spring into life when you get close, African tribal masks and fabulous aquarium.

And to really tire them out...

■ Williamson Square's new fountain, designed to be dashed through by infants of all ages (6 to 60)...
■ The Yellow Duckmarine, a 50-minute, fun-and-frolic, land-and-river tour of the waterfront and city-centre...
■ New kid's cuisine at Blue and the Pan American Bar & Grills at Albert Dock, simply younger versions of the adult menus...
■ The five-mile safari through 450 acres of parkland at Knowsley Safari Park...
■ One-hour walking tours of Liverpool's historic waterfront, starting at Albert Dock...
■ Central Library's Mystery Children's Centre with Sensory Room where kids with emotional problems can 'chill out' in a magical aquatic kingdom...
■ The mummified Egyptian crocodile at the Conservation Centre...
■ Smuggling stories at Merseyside Maritime Museum, plus the sights and sounds of emigration...
■ Hollywood Bowl at Edge Lane Retail Park, just outside the city-centre...
■ The noble lions outside St George's Hall, don't get too close or you might tread on their tails...
■ The time machine at International Space & Astronomy Centre (ISAC) by Seacombe Ferry Terminal...
■ Puppets, costumes and picture trails at the Walker's Artbase every weekend and daily from mid-July to early Sept for the school holidays...

WORLD MUSEUM Liverpool

STARS

IN THEIR EYES...

FREE ENTRY
Open Daily 10am – 5pm
www.worldmuseumliverpool.org.uk
William Brown Street, Liverpool. Tel:0151 478 4393

08 Liverpool
EUROPEAN CAPITAL OF CULTURE

Major Funders
Heritage Lottery Fund
eu&merseyside   European Funding to Develop New Opportunities   Northwest   REGIONAL DEVELOPMENT AGENCY

NATIONAL MUSEUMS LIVERPOOL

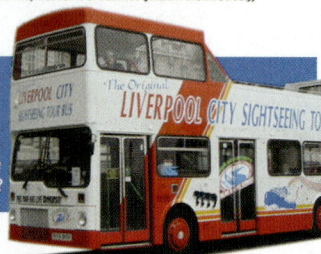

If you're here in 2005...

A nautical but nice calender and checklist for the Year of the Sea

July

■ Liverpool Summer Pops (early July) – three weeks of beautiful music down by the riverside. Macca's played here. So have Elton, Dylan, Diana Ross and Will Young.

■ Liverpool Festival of Comedy (1-17 July) – local and international gagsters aplenty over two weeks

■ Lyver Trophy Yacht Race (8 July) – gets going from Liverpool to Dublin in the qualifier for the Fastnet Race.

■ Visit of Crystal Symphony (14 July) – 50,000-ton cruise-ship visits Liverpool during its Celtic Embrace.

■ HUB Festival (mid-July) – the biggest names in BMX, skate, hip-hop and graffiti hit the waterfront.

■ Brouhaha International (July-Aug) – street events from all over the world, based on experiences of the sea (brouhaha.uk.com).

August

■ Liverpool International Beatles Week – the world's biggest annual Fab Four party, with tribute bands, guest speakers and all manner of memorabilia auctions over six days, climaxing with the massive Mathew Street Festival (27-29 Aug).

■ Honda Formula 4 Power Boat Racing (20-21 Aug) – Liverpool leg of the powerboat racing series.

■ Slavery Remembrance Day (23 Aug) – marking International Day for the Slave Trade and its Abolition.

■ Visit of Prinsendam (28 Aug) – 38,000-ton, 837-guest modern cruise-ship calls in to Liverpool.

■ Creamfields (Summer Bank Holiday 30 Aug) – the country's foremost 24-hour outdoor dancefest.

■ Liverpool Echo Entertainment Awards – Scouse superstars out in force (icliverpool.co.uk).

■ Southport Flower Show – one of the UK's largest and most famous independent floral events.

September

■ Waterfront Weekend (2-4 Sept) – music and comedy over three packed days on the Pier Head.

■ Heritage Open Days (8-11 Sept) – free access to historic buildings not usually open to the public, this year celebrating maritime architecture.

■ Southport Airshow (10-11 Sept) – one of the largest events of its kind, on the town's waterfront, with the latest military technology and aerobatic manoeuvres on display.

■ Clipper Round the World Yacht Race 2005/06 (18 Sept) – a fleet of 10 yachts sets sail from Albert Dock on an epic 11-month, 33,000-mile journey, back the following summer.

■ Liverpool Triathlon – the new Olympic sport and the ultimate test of stamina, at Albert Dock.

■ Liverpool Waterfront Classics – three nights of sweet classical music down by the river, courtesy of the Royal Liverpool Philharmonic.

■ Lord Street European Market – carnival of continental commerce.

October

■ Liverpool Echo Fashion Show – at City Exchange on Old Hall Street.

■ Run Liverpool – 10k international half-marathon through the city-centre.

■ Visit of Grand Turk (21 Oct) – replica of the magnificent 18th Century man-o-war at Albert Dock, coinciding with the 200th anniversary of the Battle of Trafalgar.

■ Liverpool Food & Drink Festival (24-31 Oct) – now in its third year, showcasing the city's wining-and-dining scene to a larger audience, with lots of yummy special events (liverpoolfoodanddrink.com).

■ Liverpool Irish Festival (late Oct) – four-day celebration of dance, drama, literature and music with free performances across the city.

November

■ City of Liverpool Fireworks Display (5 Nov) – sky ablaze over the water.

■ International Guitar Festival – acoustic heaven at various venues.

■ Christmas Lights Switch-On – with celebrities and music to light up Liverpool city-centre this Yuletide.

December

■ Liverpool Lantern Festival (early Dec) – 200 illuminated lanterns on show as part of Santa's Parade.

■ Lord Street European Market (week before Xmas) – the crepes and foie gras are back.

■ New Year's Eve Firework Display – from St George's Plateau.

■ Liverpool-New York Passengers Lists – on display at Central Library, enhancing the city's wealth of historical material (crew lists, custom records, Lloyd's Registers etc).

What's new

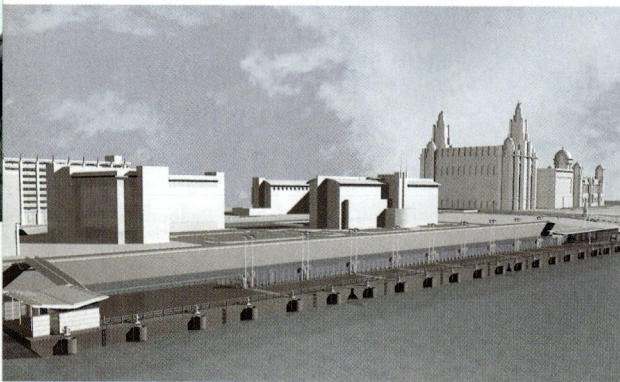

■ Welcome to a waterfront reanimated by £1billion of new developments and soon to be connected by a continuous network of walkways, improved public realm and a canal link.

It's the focal point of 120km of coastline between Southport and the Wirral – much of which is important for nature conservation – now known as the Mersey Waterfront Regional Park.

In Liverpool there'll be a £12million cruise-liner terminal (middle pic) in place by 2006, when Cunard is proposing to name a new 85,000-ton vessel in the shadow of its former headquarters. The company's first ship, the Britannia, sailed from Liverpool to North America on 4 July 1840 – and exactly 162 years later the keel of its latest vessel, the Queen Mary 2, was lowered into the building dock at St Nazaire in Brittany.

The new 2.5km canal link (top) will allow inland boats to sail from the Leeds and Liverpool Canal, past the Pier Head and into the Albert Dock. It'll include two new locks, five new bridges and a tunnel, with seating close to the water and shelter from the wind.

Further south, a world-class development at King's Dock (bottom) has been designed by architects Wilkinson & Eyre, with lots of street furniture, cafés and parks around a 9,000-seater Arena & Conference Centre and riverside walkway to the Albert Dock. The masterplan envisages 'a mixed-use waterfront quarter containing high-quality apartments, prestige hotels, and leisure and retail facilities'. Work starts now.

Architecture

The building of Liverpool. Brought to you in about, ooh, 450 words...

■ 'Architecture and sculpture are too often ignored today, partly because we no longer read the symbolism and iconography of a building as past generations were accustomed to, and also because of the very fact that it is usually subservient to an overall architectural scheme or conception...'
Gavin Stamp, Patronage and Practice: Sculpture on Merseyside. →

Best of 3...
coats of arms

■ **Compton House**, Church Street. Top of Marks and Sparks, two mermen with shell for a shield, customary Liver Birds and city motto.

■ **St George's Hall.** In semi-circular stained glass above great organ at south end, with another depicting George and Dragon in north.

■ **Mersey Travel**, 24 Hatton Garden. In granite, dating from 1907. The merman on the right should always blow a conch to summon the sea.

■ Make a fortune from shipping in the 19th Century and build a world-famous city with the proceeds. Line the docks with mighty warehouses. Express your power, pride and prestige with exuberant but dignified offices, commodity exchanges and noble banks with bronze doorways, iron balconies and exquisite sculpture. And erect rows of merchant palaces on the brow.

Specialise in Greco-Roman grandeur on a scale not seen in the provinces to create an Athens of the north. Build magnificent museums, galleries and libraries like ancient temples, and entrust a 23-year-old doomed genius to design the finest neo-classical edifice in Europe.

At the turn of the next century turn your back on the capital's Victorian aesthetic and look to the New World instead. Make breakthroughs in engineering. Use steel and concrete. Build skyscrapers that occupy whole blocks. Create a skyline like the great American cities with which you do business. Put three sisters on your waterfront, each with a character of her own: from baroque and opulent, to square and disciplined, eclectic and eccentric.

Enjoy a second Greek Revival – like nowhere else in Britain – and combine classicism with abstraction, the past with the modern. Call it 'The Liverpool Manner'. Explore Art Deco. Revisit Renaissance detail. Make an Expressionist masterpiece of a three-mile hole in the ground. Make the philharmonic, acoustic.

Then hit the brakes. Watch wartime bombing wreak wholesale devastation. See containerisation cripple the port economy. No more ships and sailors, nor exciting new buildings. But no mass demolition and brutalist redevelopment, either. And when the tide begins to change, rejoice in a fabulous architectural legacy preserved in situ – and vow to complement it with a flourish of futuristic, world-class buildings.

Experience a renaissance. Go for Heritage Site status. Become Capital of Culture. Be epic and theatrical, bold and daring once more. Be Liverpool back to her best.

■ Liverpool has 2,500 listed properties, including 26 Grade I, more than any other city outside London. Buildings that qualify: (i) those before 1700 that survive in anything like their original condition; (ii) those between 1700 and 1840 subject to selection; (iii) those between 1840 and 1914 of definite quality and character. Grade I are of exceptional interest. Grade II of special interest.

Anatomy of an art gallery

■ The Walker on William Brown Street typifies 19th-Century Liverpool's love affair with neo-classicism, combining Greek ideals of harmony with Roman advances in technology. Its portico (entrance bay) is a temple projecting from an ashlar (square-cut stone) façade. The rest is in the details…

**Best of 3…
doorways**

■ **Caffe Nero,** Castle Street. Old Adelphi Bank. Bronze doors depicting pairs of inseparable friends: Achilles and Patroclus; Castor and Pollux; Roland and Oliver.

■ **Stanley Hall,** Edmund Street. Gleaming brass on authentic Art Deco frontage, formerly home to Silcocks grain merchants.

■ **National Provincial Bank,** Water Street. Ferocious tigers whose fangs were ritually rubbed by Indian sailors for good luck.

■ **Pediment:** triangular roof surmounting the portico, with tympanum (often featuring reliefs or busts) at its centre.

■ **Cornice:** horizontal decorative projection, here running along pediment and crowning entablature.

■ **Entablature:** upper part of portico or entrance bay, supported by columns and including cornice.

■ **Capital:** stylised elaboration at top of column, typically acanthus leaves (spiky shrub common in Mediterranean countries).

■ **Shaft:** slender part of column.

■ **Pedestal:** plinth and dado (square slab) supporting base of column.

■ **Frieze:** horizontal band of decorative sculpture along walls of façade.

■ **Corinthian column:** one of five types of classical column, with fluted shaft and decorated capital, and used by Romans. The other four are: Doric (simplest Greek order – see Wellington's Column); Ionic (Greek with scrolls either side of capital – see Oratory next to Anglican Cathedral); Tuscan (least ornamented); and Composite (mixing Corinthian and Ionic).

The neo-classical Church of St Bride
on Percy Street (Hope Quarter)

One in a mullion

**Best of 3...
domes**

■ **Town Hall,** Castle Street. Dizzyingly beautiful blue, white and gold decoration inside, with city motto and history of building in large gilded letters along the base.

■ **Port of Liverpool Building,** Pier Head. You shouldn't really stick one on top of Renaissance palace. But who cares? Glorious.

■ **Lyceum Building,** Bold Street. Sub-Sistine splendour for diners in Prohibition's restaurant, formerly home to Post Office.

■ Most people wouldn't give it a second glance, but no16 Cook Street was one of 40 Liverpool locations open to the public over the last Heritage Weekend. On the narrow thoroughfare trundling down fom Castle Street to Victoria Street, it doesn't look like a 'normal' office building at all – more like a giant church window minus the stained glass, a huge pane with three arches divided by slender stone mullions or vertical bars. Inside is pretty impressive, too, with a beautiful, cast-iron spiral staircase enclosed on the outside by a tall glass cylinder best viewed from the rear courtyard. The staircase has 69 steps, twisting from top to bottom through four storeys.

Pretty amazing stuff for 1866 – the date it was built to the specifications of architect Peter Ellis, who also designed the equally dazzling, Grade I listed Oriel Chambers on Water Street three years earlier. Neither was appreciated in its day, with one critic from The Builder, the foremost English architectural periodical of the 19th Century, damning Oriel Chambers as 'a vast

abortion which would be depressing were it not ludicrous'. But today both buildings are regarded as modernist icons because they break away from classical tradition and predate the same kind of glazed commercial structures in America by a good two decades.

In fact, there's an intriguing link with one of Chicago's oldest and most famous high-rise buildings. Dating from 1888, the Rookery was designed by Daniel Burnham and John Root and boasts its own, very similar spiral staircase. Root spent time in Liverpool as a teenager after his father smuggled him out of America during the Civil War – just as no16 and Oriel Chambers were going up.

Coincidence? On the message board of a website called skyscrapercity.com, a member wrote: 'There was a stunned silence from my cousin's Chicago-born husband when he visited Cook Street last year. Chicagoans are brought up from birth thinking they invented everything to do with skyscrapers, so he was shocked to learn that in this case they had merely slavishly copied Liverpool'.

The glass cylinder enclosing the spiral
staircase at the rear of no16 Cook Street

Let there be light

■ Walk down Princes Street in the Business District, hang a right down Roe Alley towards North John Street and you might think you've been transported to the Middle East – or at least the set of Indiana Jones & The Last Crusade. There, ahead of you and framed by the alley's gorge-like walls, is Liverpool's equivalent of the temple at Petra, the wonder of the ancient world hewn from the pink cliffs of the desert.

Except this isn't Jordanian rock, it's Portland Stone – cladding two of the six great ventilation shafts designed by Herbert Rowse for the Queensway Tunnel in the 1930s, and used for several other fine buildings in the city as well as St Paul's Cathedral in London.

Quarried for centuries from the eponymous peninsula in Dorset, it's a 200million-year-old limestone composed of fossilised shell creatures and famous for its capacity to absorb and reflect light. Carving it – say the experts – is like cutting into a block of light, creating darkness with each cut of the chisel and even producing rhythmic sound waves through its brittle granular structure. A simple, stunningly beautiful building material, as our Indy would no doubt agree.

Green and serene

Relax. In town and off the beaten park there are plenty of oases of tranquillity...

Best of 3...
urban retreats

■ **Bluecoat Courtyard**, off School Lane. Rustic haven in one of Liverpool's oldest buildings, slap-bang in the middle of the Shopping Centre.

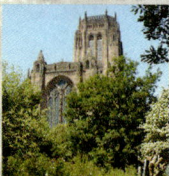

■ **St James Gardens**, Anglican Cathedral. Home to wild roses, native and exotic, like the Burnet, Abyssinia, Damask, Tibetan and Old Blush.

■ **St John's Gardens**, behind St George's Hall. Former church site in the Cultural Quarter, laid out as terraced gardens 100 years ago.

■ A big, brawny city on a windswept coast with miles upon miles of gritty docklands – and one million trees and over 2,500 acres of parks and open spaces. Sounds almost too good to be true. Sounds just like Liverpool.

The great swathes of Stanley Park and Newsham Park (both east of the city centre) and Sefton Park (to the south) are a legacy from late Victorian days when Liverpool's great and good had the foresight – in the nick of time – to create green lungs and leafy arteries for a city seething and sprawling with humanity.

For years the cherished notion had been to build a city as beautiful as Florence. A century on, Liverpudlians are beginning to appreciate again how lucky they are. Five of the city's parks are included on the English Heritage Register of Historic Parks as Grade II sites and eight have been awarded Green Flag status by the Civic Trust.

Chavasse Park, close to the waterfront, is being re-landscaped as part of the massive Paradise Street project and the city has its own National Wildflower Centre set in a tranquil park in Knowsley (just off the M62). Check out its well-stocked shop and the wonderful 160-metre rooftop walkway.

Liverpool is championing not just conservation but ecology, too. At Croxteth Hall & Country Park (north-east) a former estate has been transformed into 400 acres of woodland and farm with a Victorian walled garden. And last year the Merseyside Caribbean Centre on Parliament Street unveiled a wildflower garden containing mosaic flags of the six West Indian islands made from coloured glass chippings, to coincide with the first annual National Recycling Week.

Sefton Park, 132 years old and the grandest of all the green spaces, is awash with joggers these days and stages mass events like the annual Liverpool Women's 10k Run. But it still harbours corners of peace and quiet amid its 200 acres of mature forest trees.

Designed by local architect Louis Hornblower and Edouard André, a Parisian pupil of Napoleon III's landscape gardener, it's a fairytale landscape of curved pathways, streams with stepping stones and bridges, grottos and gateways, ornamental buildings and a boating lake. In spring, along its sweeping oval edge, there really is a host of golden daffodils, as well as carpets of brilliant bluebells.

A couple of miles east is Calderstones, now home to the Liverpool International Tennis Tournament and a 125-acre Eden named after a stone formation dating back 4,000 years. Like Sefton Park, it has its own lake and glasshouse, plus a Japanese flower garden with koi carp in a lily-covered pond. There's also a dog-free picnic area and children's playground opened by Paul McCartney in memory of his late wife Linda. The colossal figures either side of the entrance gates are Atlantes – carvings of the Titan in Greek mythology who held up the pillars of the Universe.

You can explore all of these beautiful parks with Liverpool Rangers, who offer a wide range of walks, talks and organised events, most of which are free of charge (0151 225 5910). This may be a football-mad city split down the middle between rabid Reds and loyal Blues, but there's definitely a growing army of fanatical Greens.

Story of the Palm House

■ The Grade II listed jewel in Sefton Park's crown was a gift from millionaire Henry Yates Thompson in 1896. It measures 100ft in diameter and rises 82 feet in three glazed tiers from an octagonal base of red granite from the Isle of Mull. Shattered by an incendiary bomb during the Second World War, it was painstakingly restored by a group of local residents and is once again a major botanical and events attraction.

2. Business District

4. Cultural Quarter

3. Shopping Centre

1. Pier Head & Albert Dock

6. Hope Quarter

5. Rope Walks

Walk this way

The city-centre of Liverpool. In six easy sections...

■ Liverpool city-centre is easily subdivided into six walkable areas, each with their own distinct identity: the maritime Pier Head and Albert Dock, commercial and architecturally-important Business District, retail-led Shopping Centre, neo-classical Cultural Quarter, dynamic Rope Walks and idyllic Hope Quarter. Follow the trail in depth over the next 50 pages – there's a map for each area and information about local landmarks and other points of interest. Plus some rather nice pictures, we'd like to think...

space

Stylish **living** in **Liverpool**

Liverpool. The **life.** The **style.** Every two months. **For free.**

1.

Pier Head and Albert Dock

■ What better place to start than the iconic water's edge? Top of the tourist ticklist, the Pier Head is dominated by the familiar mirages of the Royal Liver, Cunard and Port of Liverpool buildings, known as the Graces after three daughters of Zeus who represented splendour, festivity and abundance (see John Gibson's sculpture in the Walker Gallery). A spectacular new Museum of Liverpool is on the way. This is a wonderfully walkable area, book-ended by the exciting developments at Prince's Dock and myriad attractions of Albert Dock, and soon to be joined up by a cruise-liner terminal and canal link.

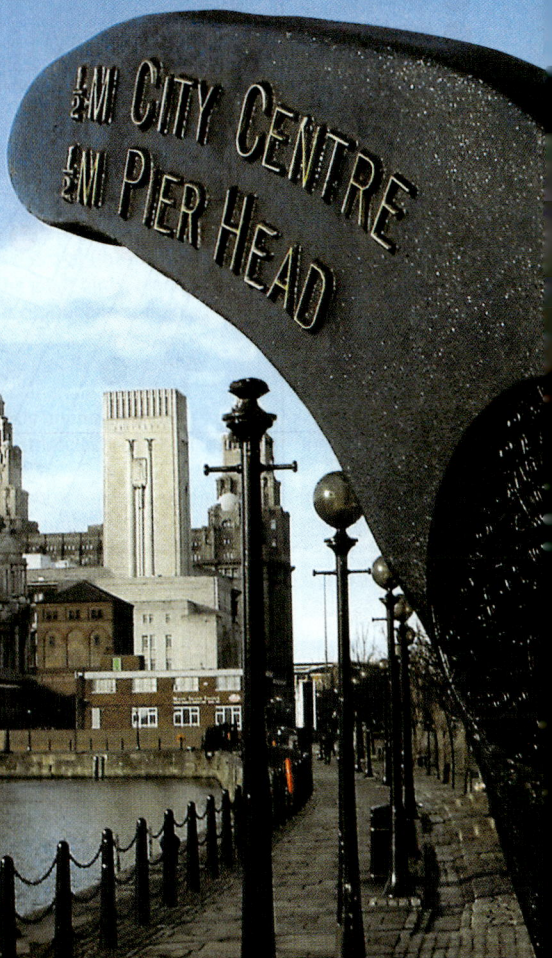

George's Dock Building

■ Another Art Deco masterpiece by Herbert Rowse (see the Martins Bank Building and Philharmonic Hall), dating from 1934 and, for many, the original Fourth Grace. Its monolithic shape was inspired, some say, by Howard Carter's excavations in Egypt a decade earlier, but is there a touch of Flash Gordon about the futuristic details?

At the base are two figures in black basalt symbolising Night and Day, and all four sides of the central shaft of the building feature decorative panels flanked by sculptured Liver Birds nesting on columns. There's also a 7ft high relief called Speed: the Modern Mercury (wearing a racing helmet and goggles) plus four more figures representing Civil Engineering, Construction, Architecture and Decoration and holding, respectively, a cross-section of a tunnel, model of trabeation (beams used in construction), Ionic capital and Assyrian capital with back-to-back crouching bulls.

Then as now, the building provides a fabulous contrast to the dominant Victorian gothic and neo-classical architecture of Liverpool. And to think its sole function is to pump used air out of the Mersey Tunnel.

(K)night...

And Day

Lusitania propeller

Eye eye...

■ Planned for summer 2005, the world's newest revolving Eye will stand 197ft (that's equivalent to 15 double decker buses) above Canning Half-Tide Dock (near Albert Dock), overlooking the river with views of the UNESCO World Heritage Site, North Wales and the Irish Sea. Weighing 345 tonnes and supported by tanks containing 40,000 gallons of water, it'll revolve three times per ride, with 42 'see pods' each accommodating eight people (336 people per ride). Fitted with climate control and air-conditioning, and taking one week to transport and construct, the Eye would also help light up the city's world-famous skyline at night, with 60,000 LEDs along its 21 huge steel spokes. It'll be open 10am to 11pm, seven days a week.

■ One of four 23-ton propellers from the Cunard liner Lusitania, which was torpedoed by a German U-Boat off southern Ireland in May 1915 while returning to Liverpool from New York. One of the largest and most luxurious ships afloat, the Lusitania left the Mersey on her maiden voyage to America in 1907, the propellers rotating at three times a second and driving the ship across the Atlantic at over 26 knots (30mph). Her sinking caused the loss of 1,201 lives and precipitated the USA's entry into the First World War.

Albert Dock

■ You're now approaching the largest group of Grade I listed buildings in England – one of the earliest enclosed docks in the world and something akin to a waterfront castle. A triumph of function and design, they were conceived in 1846 by Jesse Hartley (the city's Dock Engineer) and consist of five formidable warehouses – check out the sheer bulk of their sandstone and granite slabs – each five storeys high with a combined capacity of 250,000 tons. 'Strong, masculine buildings, sleeves rolled up and muscles bulging', as one local history book describes them. They were almost demolished in the 1980s to make way for a car park. Today the whole area is a conservation site embracing Tate Liverpool, the Maritime Museum, Beatles Story, bars and restaurants, shops and flats, adjacent docks, swing bridges, watchmen's huts and pier master's house. And what about those vistas...

Bird? Plane? No, Albert Duck

Introducing...

Premier Travel Inn

■ What's the best thing about Premier Travel Inn on Vernon Street? Maybe it's the location in the heart of Liverpool's Business District, two minutes away from the Shopping Centre and bars. Or it could be the welcoming team, express check-out, fully modernised and secure NCP car park just opposite the hotel, Wi-Fi wireless internet access and superb range of meeting rooms (with air cooling, natural daylight, direct-dial telephones and state -of-the-art audio visual aid).

Then again, it might be the fact that all rooms have luxurious double-beds, ensuite bathrooms , spacious desks with telephones and modem points, tea and coffee making facilities, Sky TV, special designs for customers with disabilities, and black-out curtains. Or perhaps it's just the 100 per cent Satisfaction Guarantee – if you're not completely satisfied, we don't expect you to pay. Amazing value at £52.95 midweek and £55.95 weekends. **Call 0870 238 3323 now.**

2. Business District

■ Wander up James Street or Water Street from the Pier Head and the whiff of commerce hits you straightaway. There are several modern developments, notably in and around Old Hall Street, but the traditional architecture of the Business District is overwhelmingly Victorian – with the occasional, glorious Art Deco intrusion. It's a reaction to the growth of Liverpool's docks in the preceding decades, with rows of elegant premises along the city's seven original streets (Dale, Water, Tithebarn, Chapel, Old Hall, High and Castle). Many of these buildings were once banks or exchanges for every form of commodity from cotton to corn to fruit, and the whole district is rich in symbolism and steeped in history – if you know just where to look.

2. Business District

The attractions...

- **FL** Face of Liverpool
- **LE** Liverpool Daily Post & Echo
- **UL** Unity Living
- **CE** Cotton Exchange
- **RP** Rumford Place
- **PC** Parish Church
- **MB** Martins Bank
- **TH** Town Hall
- **EX** Exchange Station
- **AH** Albion House
- **BE** Bank of England
- **NV** North John Street Ventilation Tower
- **SS** Sanctuary Stone

The hotels...

1. Sir Thomas Hotel
2. Premier Travel Inn
3. Radisson SAS
4. Thistle
5. Racquet Club

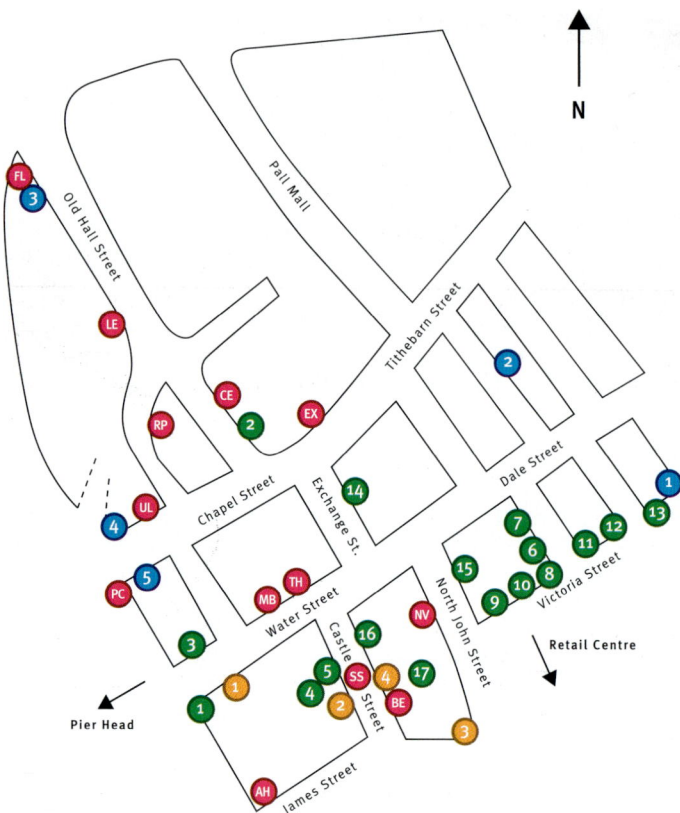

N

Old Hall Street

Pall Mall

Tithebarn Street

Chapel Street

Exchange St.

Dale Street

Water Street

Castle Street

North John Street

Victoria Street

James Street

Pier Head

Retail Centre

City Exchange

■ Home to the Liverpool Daily Post & Echo, the city's morning and evening newspapers, and one of the best modern frontages in Liverpool. The light and spacious, multi-level atrium provides enhanced access from the street and stages everything from photo-graphic exhibitions to private parties and trade fairs under its stunning tubular canopy.

Is there an Echo in here?

Get the bales in

Cotton Exchange

■ The ornate Edwardian façade may have gone, but this place is steeped in history. It's the headquarters of the Liverpool Cotton Association, opened in 1906 by the Prince and Princess of Wales (their signatures are on the opening page of the priceless visitor's book). Back then, 5million bales of raw cotton were imported to Liverpool every year. Today, over 60 per cent of the world's cotton is still traded under LCA rules. Outside the Exchange is an alleorical statue of the River Mersey, and in the courtyard are two statues of Navigation and Commerce, the only survivors of eight that once stood high up on the roof.

Face of Liverpool

■ At the foot of 30-storey Beetham Tower (with a twin structure called West Tower on its way) is this captivating urban art project that celebrates the area's history and context. A triangular garden site, it uses geometry, symbols and maps to evoke travel and adventure, while 32 blue discs within the walls portray contemporary faces reflecting Liverpool's ethnic diversity.

The bars and restaurants...

1 Simply Heathcotes
2 Albany Dining Rooms
3 Newz Bar
4 Slaughterhouse
5 Franco's
6 Algarve
7 Casa Italia
8 Superstar Boudoir
9 Metro
10 Pacific Bar & Grill
11 Living Room
12 Don Pepe
13 Sultan's Palace
14 Anderson's
15 La Vina
16 Olive Press
17 Piccolino

The shops...

1 Circa 1900 Antiques
2 Bang & Olufsen
3 Boodle & Dunthorne
4 Andrew Collinge

The Albany

■ One of the jewels in Liverpool's crown of listed buildings, famous for its courtyard and cast-iron staircases, and just re-opened on Old Hall Street as a complex of apartments with the sumptuous Albany Dining Rooms at basement level. It was originally built in 1858 for Richard Naylor, a wealthy banker and philanthropist, and his initials are carved into the exterior stonework. The architect was JK Colling, a Londoner with a passion for flower drawing who later designed the National Portrait Gallery near Trafalgar Square, and whose lithographs from his book Details of Gothic Architecture are popular as posters today.

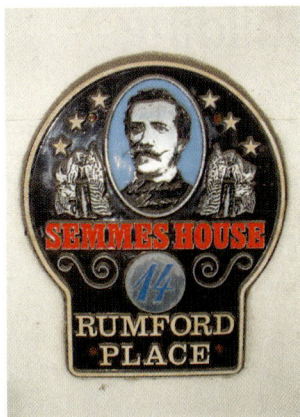

Where Bulloch broke the Union blockade

It happened here...

■ Rumford Place is the little corner of Liverpool that's forever America. The Star Spangled Banner recalls its former incarnation, at the outbreak of the US Civil War 140 years ago, as the premises of Charleston cotton merchants, John Fraser and Co. With two-thirds of American cotton coming through Liverpool they were also the European bankers for the Confederacy. When the Union threw a blockade around Confederate ports in 1861, Captain James Bulloch was sent secretly from Georgia to England with $1milion to build ships that would break the siege. He stayed at Rumford Place and, with the aid of fellow agent Isidor Straus (an American immigrant originally from Georgia in the Caucasus), financed the construction of 35 'raiders' – most notoriously the Alabama that destroyed or captured over 60 Union vessels. The last surrender of the war was made on 6 November 1865 by his final ship, the Shenandoah, on the Mersey – but to the British government rather than the Union. Bulloch was denied amnesty by the US and remained in Liverpool for the rest of his life. He died in 1901 and was buried at Toxteth Cemetery. Straus was allowed to return home, eventually buying Macy's department store in New York and becoming one of the world's richest men. He died on the Titanic in 1912 and was buried at Woodlawn Cemetery in the Bronx. Rumford Place had another visitor in 1958. By then it was home to the Mercantile Marine Service Association, which was approached by a retired mariner trying to clear his name upon the release of the movie A Night To Remember. Stanley Lord had been captain of the Californian, the ship bound for Boston from Liverpool that reportedly ignored the Titanic's distress signals. He died four years later, aged 84, at his home in Wallasey on the Wirral.

Albion House

■ A beautiful building on the corner of the Strand and James Street, with alternating bands of red brick and Portland Stone (the architect Richard Shaw also designed New Scotland Yard in London). It was built for the Oceanic Steam Navigation Company, or White Star Line, and it was here that many of the crew of the Titanic were enlisted. It was here, too, that their relatives converged, desperate for news when the ship sank in April 1912.

Martins Bank Building

■ A truly great Liverpool building, it's actually one of the finest realisations of early American commercial architecture in the UK. Designed for the old Martins Bank in 1932 by Herbert Rowse (the genius behind the India Building, Philharmonic Hall and George's Dock Building), its exterior is decorated with maritime motifs and Liver Birds topped by grasshoppers – a reference to the name of the London tavern where a moneylender practised the country's first banking system in the late 16th century. The eighth-floor boardroom is just as fabulous, with a walnut ceiling swimming in mermaids, dolphins, seahorses and starfish. During the Second World War the building stored Britain's gold bullion reserves for shipment to Canada should the country be invaded, and it's been home to Barclays since 1969.

Building of interest in more ways than one

Bank of England Building

■ Grade I listed and designed by Charles Cockerill, who also finished St George's Hall after the untimely death of Harvey Lonsdale Elmes (see Cultural Quarter). Striking in appearance and classically Greek in detail, it looks bigger than it is – which is exactly what the architect intended.

Parish Church

■ Full name, the Church of Our Lady and St Nicholas. Because the latter is also the patron saint of seaman, it's also known as the Sailor's Church. A lunchtime retreat for office workers, with bags of history – victims of the Plague were buried here in 1361 (but don't let that put you off your sandwiches)a nd during the English Civil War, both sides used it to detain prisoners. The Mersey used to reach its stone walls at high tide, which is why the dock road here is called Strand, meaning a shoreline (see also the tiny street called Sea Brow on the other side of James Street).

3.
Shopping
Centre

■ The hub of Liverpool's six walking zones may be retail-based, but it has just as much to offer in terms of the arts, heritage and architecture. Woolworth's, for example, opened its first British store on Church Street in 1909. On the site next door, Harrods seriously considered setting up shop 15 years later, actually commissioning a design from the day's leading architects. And in how many other shopping centres around the UK would you find a Big Willie stuck to the outside of a major department store? Look out, too, for the birthplace of a popular 60s musical act called The Beatles. Wonder whatever became of them...

3. Shopping Centre

N ↑

The attractions...

- OB Observatory
- CC Conservation Centre
- WS Williamson Square
- PT Playhouse Theatre
- SB St. John's Beacon
- NT Neptune Theatre
- AT Athenaeum
- BC Bluecoat Chambers
- WC PCT Walk-in Centre
- 08 08 Place

The hotels...

- 1 Marriot City
- 2 Holiday Inn

The bars and restaurants...

- 1 Orchid Spring
- 2 Puccino's
- 3 Grapes
- 4 Dr. Duncan's
- 5 Queen Square (Honey Harmony, Ask, La Tasca etc)

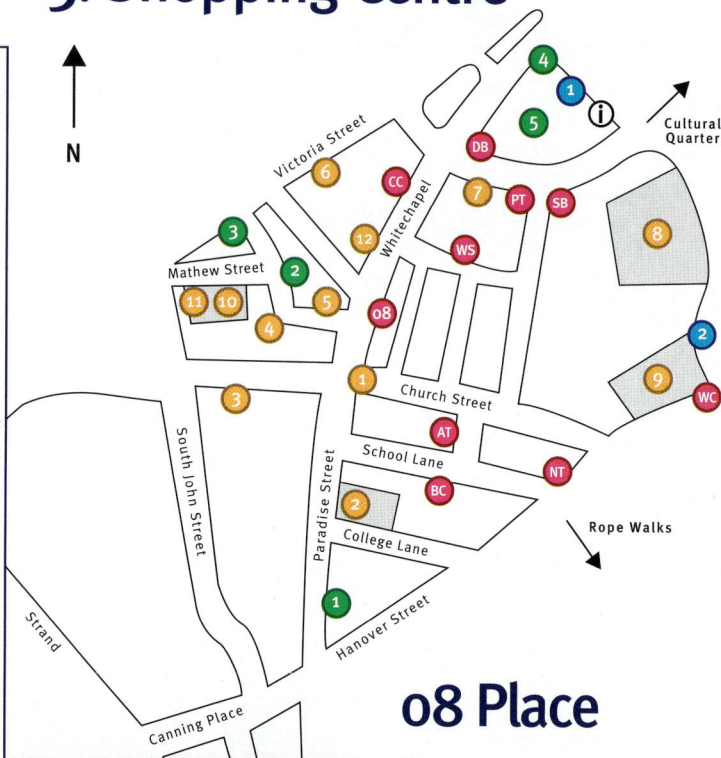

Cultural Quarter

Victoria Street

Mathew Street

Whitechapel

South John Street

Paradise Street

School Lane

Church Street

College Lane

Strand

Canning Place

Hanover Street

Rope Walks

08 Place

■ The World in One City, pretty much in one building. Welcome to a first port-of-call for visitors to Liverpool (a short walk from Mathew Street, opposite the new Met Quarter retail development on Whitechapel), a new cultural centre showcasing the Capital of Culture Experience in the build-up to 2008 and beyond and offering a huge range of services – including a ticketing and booking office, official merchandise, tourist information and details about forthcoming and future events. Easy to reach and use as a base, with the proposed city-centre tram route including a stop directly opposite the building.

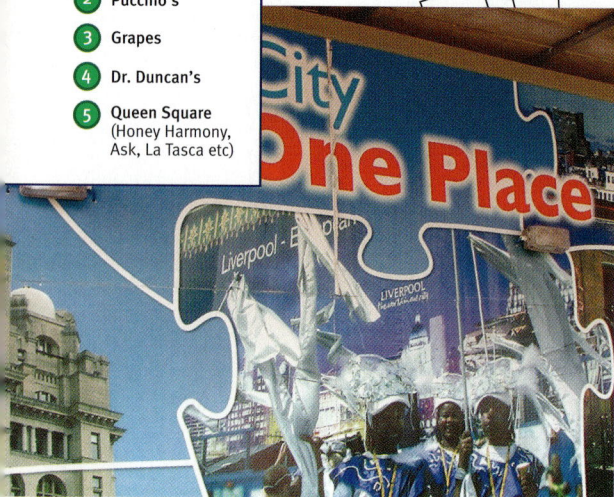

It happened here...

■ Music. Liverpool. Mathew Street. This is history, folks, the real deal. Ready? From the North John Street entrance, the first statue is a life-size Lennon dressed in leather jacket over roll-neck sweater and jeans, leaning against a doorway (from the cover of his 1975 album Rock 'n' Roll). Next to him is the Wall of Fame, unveiled in 1997 to celebrate the 40th anniversary of the opening of the Cavern Club, the old site of which is just across the road (The Rolling Stones, The Who, Chuck Berry, Rod Stewart and Stevie Wonder also played here). The Wall features the name of every one of Liverpool's 54 No1 chart hits since 1952 (it's in the Guinness Book of Records as the World Capital of Pop). Nearby, Four Lads Who Shook the World, a sculpture by Arthur Dooley of 'Mother Liverpool' holding Paul, George and Ringo, with John wearing a halo to the right. Inside Cavern Walks is John Doubleday's more conventional Beatles statue, and further down the street, above The Beatles Shop, is a bronze bust of the band entitled From Us To You, by David Hughes.

The shops...

1. **Church Steet** (BHS, Gap, Boots, JJB Sports, Marks & Spencer, John Lewis, Open, Littlewoods, Dorothy Perkins, Burtons, Top Shop, HMV, Next, WH Smith etc)
2. **Quiggins Centre**
3. **Sevenoaks Sound & Vision**
4. **Wade Smith**
5. **Reiss**
6. **Designer City**
7. **Liverpool FC Superstore**
8. **St John's Centre**
9. **Clayton Square**
10. **Cavern Walks** (Cricket, Paloma, Arrogant Cat, Drome etc)
11. **Vivienne Westwood**
12. **Met Quarter**

Wearing the face that she keeps in a jar by the door

Eleanor Rigby

■ Bronze sculpture (temporarily housed behind Mathew Street while the new Met Quarter is built) dedicated to 'All the Lonely People' and presented to Liverpool in 1982. Her creator Tommy Steele (the very same) placed a comic, page from the Bible, four-leaf clover, pair of football boots and four love sonnets inside the figure, so she'd "be full of magical properties." Eleanor Rigby was on a headstone in a church cemetery in Woolton where John and Paul first met.

Church Street

■ Some fine classical buildings on the city's main shopping artery. Compton House (above), now home to Marks and Spencer, was originally a draper's store then a hotel (you can just make out the name in the top right corner of the old picture, below left). It was designed in 1867 by Gerald de Courcy Fraser, who was also the architect for the adjacent John Lewis building on Basnett Street constructed just after the First World War. Yes, that really is a Mark I tank, or 'Big Willie', protruding from the wall.

Bluecoat Chambers

■ At the end of Church Alley is the city-centre's oldest building and arguably its most elegant. It was built by a sea captain and an inscription on the outside reads: 'Dedicated to the promotion of Christian charity and the training of poor boys in the principles of the Anglican Church. Founded this year of salvation 1717'. Now home to the Bluecoat Arts and Display Centres, with a tree-lined courtyard and new wing housing a gallery and performance space under construction.

The Great Escape

■ One of Liverpool's most intriguing landmarks, weighing over three tons and created by Edward Cronshaw, whose figurative work shows Mexican and Romanesque influences and is a reaction against 'dimensional and decorative' modern sculpture. A horse, a man and a popular rendezvous for shoppers and pigeons.

Williamson Square

■ Handy stop-off for tired feet and home to the legendary Playhouse Theatre (the most recent Liverpool building to be listed, more specifically its new glazed extensions in 1975 and 1999 respectively) and now a fountain that produces a double-arch of water and blaze of changing colours at night. Inlaid around it is a poem by Roger McGough, written to be read from any point ('Water is Liverpool is river is paradox'). We also recommend a stroll along nearby Richmond Street – everything from sandwiches to leather jackets to watch repairs to stationary, all under a plethora of architectural styles.

St John's Beacon

■ Towering over the cityscape at 450ft high, this was once a restaurant and is now the HQ of Radio City. Near its base is the St John's Shopping Centre on the site of the old St John's Market, itself a beautiful building with 130 arched window-bays that was captured for posterity by watercolour artist Samuel Austin in 1827. In the painting below (on display at the Lady Lever Gallery on the Wirral) are two black figures – a page and woman worker – suggesting that arrivals from Africa and the Americas had become a relatively integrated part of Liverpool life by the early 19th Century.

Athenaeum

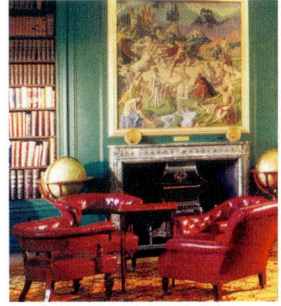

■ On Church Alley, before Bluecoat Chambers, is the only Liverpool 'newsroom' still in existence – a private club founded in 1797 as 'a meeting place where ideas could be exchanged in pleasant surroundings'. Its library (60,000 items, including the historic Roscoe Collection bought on the celebrated Liverpool philanthropist's behalf) was remarked upon by American author Washington Irvine in 1848 and is now used as a film and TV location. Today the club is hired for functions and parties.

Liverpool Resurgent

■ Striding forward on the prow of a ship jutting over the entrance to Lewis's department store on Ranelagh Street (opposite the Adelphi Hotel) and known locally as Dickie Lewis for fairly self-evident reasons. He was created in 1954 by sculptor Jacob Epstein (born in New York, studied with Rodin in Paris) to symbolise the city's indomitability after 68 air raids during the Second World War. Note, too, the reliefs of post-war Liverpool children at play underneath.

Paradise found...

■ Two centuries ago Paradise Street was 'Sailortown', a warren of taverns, grog shops, seaman's digs and brothels. Today it's the epicentre of Europe's biggest retail project, all £750million of it, linking Albert Dock to Rope Walks and scheduled for completion in 2007. Paradise Street itself will be pedestrian boulevard of high-street stores. Nearby Hanover Street will have a lifestyle focus, while South John Street will be family-oriented. Chavasse Park will be recreated as The Park (a five-acre open terraced space), and Canning Place will be the transport interchange for buses and Merseytram. Meanwhile, where Paradise Street crosses into Whitechapel, the prestigious new Met Quarter is taking shape. This from the same developers with a stake in Barcelona's spectacular Maremagnum retail centre, so expect it to be a little bit special.

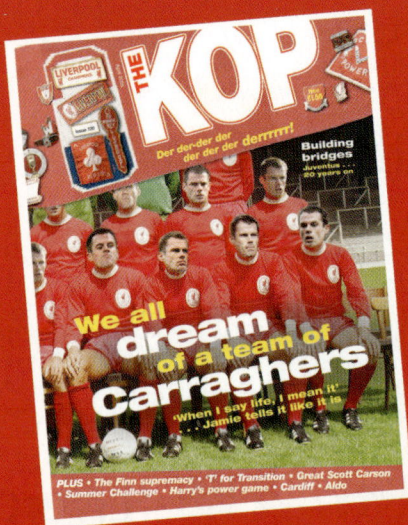

4. Cultural Quarter

■ Welcome to what the Pevsner architectural guide to Liverpool hails as 'a piece of romantic classical urban scenery [with] no equal in England'. William Brown Street (originally Shaw's Brow and home to windmills, a lunatic asylum and pottery industry) was named after an Irish cotton trader who emigrated to America in 1800 then settled in Liverpool 12 years later, financing the construction of the city's first museum and library. Already, St George's Hall had been opened and the quarter was earmarked as a cultural 'forum'. The nearby Royal Alexandra Theatre & Opera House on Lime Street was erected in 1866 and replaced by the Empire Theatre in 1925 (we insist you take in the brilliant view from the café-bar). The seven-storey North Western Hotel (now student accommodation) was designed in 1871 by Alfred Waterhouse – the same architect behind London's Natural History Museum. And the train station, at one end of the world's first true public railway, boasted the world's first iron shed with the world's largest arched span (200ft). Breath-taking stuff, we think you'll agree.

4. Cultural Quarter

The attractions...

- **LM** Liverpool Museum
- **CL** Central Library
- **WG** Walker Art Gallery
- **CS** County Sessions House
- **WC** Wellington's Column & Steble Fountain
- **QT** Queensway Tunnel
- **SG** St George's Hall
- **CT** Cenotaph
- **SJ** St John's Gardens
- **ET** Empire Theatre
- **CA** Carling Academy
- **LS** Lime Street Station

The hotels...

- **1** Gladstone
- **2** Travelodge

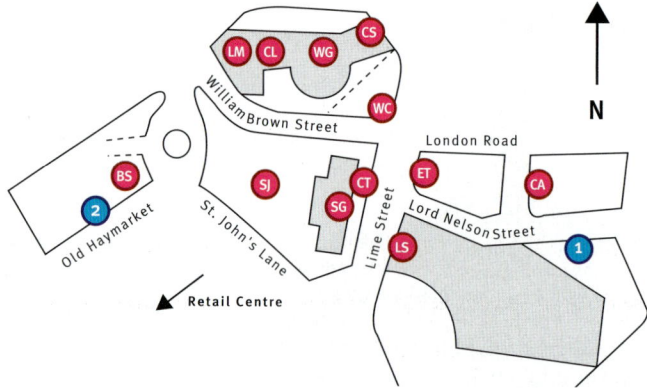

Map labels: William Brown Street, London Road, Old Haymarket, St. John's Lane, Lime Street, Lord Nelson Street, Retail Centre, N

World Museum

■ Now the stunning World Museum, in 1860 it was simply Liverpool Museum – the first of the William Brown Street buildings, and delivered in the same Greco-Roman style as St George's Hall which had stood for 15 years. An annexe, originally housing a Technical School, was added in 1901. Above its entrance is a symbolic sculpture of Liverpool holding a globe and sceptre, and note the seahorses on the bronze lamp standards by the corner of Byrom Street, designed by Frederick Pomeroy. Believe it or not, he went on to design the first Mr Universe statuette in America.

It happened here...

■ On 18 July 1934, King George V and Queen Mary officially opened Queensway, designed by Herbert Rowse as the longest underwater road tunnel in the world and a deliberately modernist contrast to the neo-classical style of the Cultural Quarter's grand buildings. Queensway even has its own coat of arms. Between two giant winged bulls ('symbolic of swift and heavy traffic') stand Apollo and Pluto, the gods of light and darkness. The shield between them contains a Liver Bird and two stars below two lions holding a wheel. The motto underneath is Ripae Ulterioris Amore. It's from Virgil's Aeneid and means, 'In longing for the further bank'.

Central Library

■ Built in conjunction with the Museum, this was the first original free library in the country. Today it has 600,000 visitors every year. The drum-shaped Picton Reading Room, following the curve in the street and modelled on the British Museum Reading Room, was added in 1879 and became the first building in the city to have electric lighting. By 2008, Central Library will be reinvented as a World Discovery Centre connected to the Museum and Walker by an internal walkway, with its 90million archives on Liverpool's history digitised to create an online genealogy service linked to Ellis Island Visitor Centre in New York.

The Walker

■ The first major public art gallery outside London, styled as a Roman temple and named after the local brewer who paid for its construction in 1870. The seated statues of Michelangelo (right and overleaf) and Raphael, representing sculpture and painting, were carved by John Warrington Wood in Italy. In 1876 the Liverpool Mercury noted that the Michelangelo was 'gazing upwards as if to contemplate some work maturing itself into imagined existence'. The allegorical Liverpool on the roof is a copy of his original, now in the Conservation Centre.

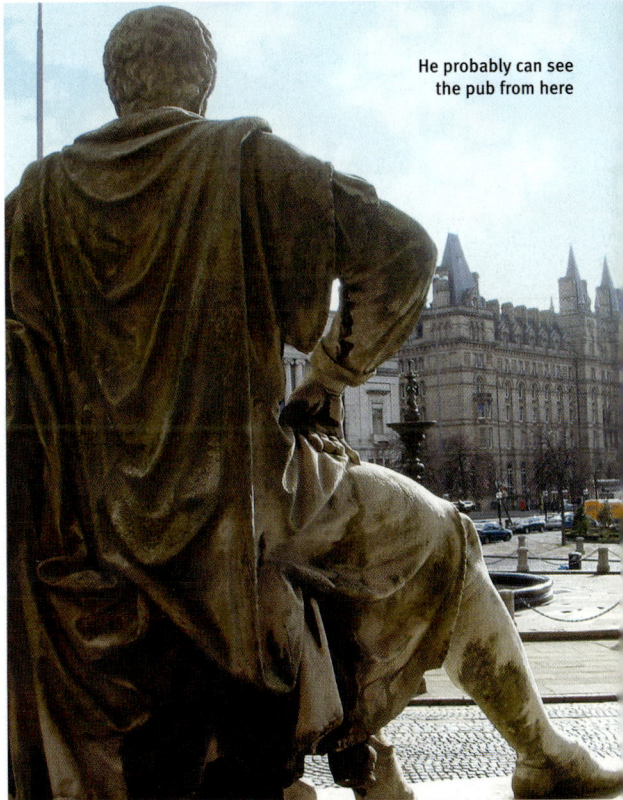

He probably can see the pub from here

St John's Gardens

■ A sloping, tranquil terrace, opened in 1904 on the grounds of a former church from which it takes its name. There are several monuments to Liverpool's great and good (among them William Gladstone) and many of the city's 30 war memorials are here (including one to 357 members of the King's Liverpool Regiment lost in Afghanistan, Burma and South Africa). More recently a memorial was unveiled to commemorate the 60th anniversary of D-Day.

County Sessions House

■ The last of the set, opened in 1884 and featuring four pairs of Corinthian columns and the Lancashire coat of arms on its pediment. There's a fine Italian Renaissance staircase inside, but you'll have to wait till the next Heritage Open Day (every September) to see it.

Steble Fountain

■ Unveiled in 1879 as a gift to the city from its mayor, RF Steble. The cast-iron figures around the base are Neptune, Amphitrite (his wife), Acis (a river deity) and Galatea (sea nymph). It's a copy of an original designed by Paul Lienard for the Paris World Fair of 1855. There's another version outside Massachusetts State House in Boston as well as replicas in Lyon, Bordeaux, Geneva and Cairo.

St George's Hall

■ The royal favourite. On a tour of Liverpool in 1851, Queen Victoria said it was "worthy of ancient Athens, the architecture is so simple and magnificent." More recently Prince Charles called it "one of the greatest public buildings of the last 200 years which sits in the centre of one of Europe's finest cities."

This 490ft long, neo-classical masterpiece was designed by 23-year-old Harvey Lonsdale Elmes, who died in the West Indies a decade later from consumption. The Great Hall's 7,737-pipe organ is the third largest in the UK (after London's Albert Hall and Liverpool's Anglican Cathedral), and the exquisite, once-covered sunken floor of blue and brown tiles is now partially glazed for viewing.

Above all, it's an emphatic declaration of the city's status as the second city of the British Empire. On the six pairs of bronze doors inside are the letters SPQL, an adaptation of the motto of Rome and meaning 'to the Senate and the People of Liverpool'. Outside, a pride of four lions, each 14ft long, stand guard while the building completes an £18m refurbishment. Several historic rooms have been restored, and a brand new visitor centre will be open by 2007.

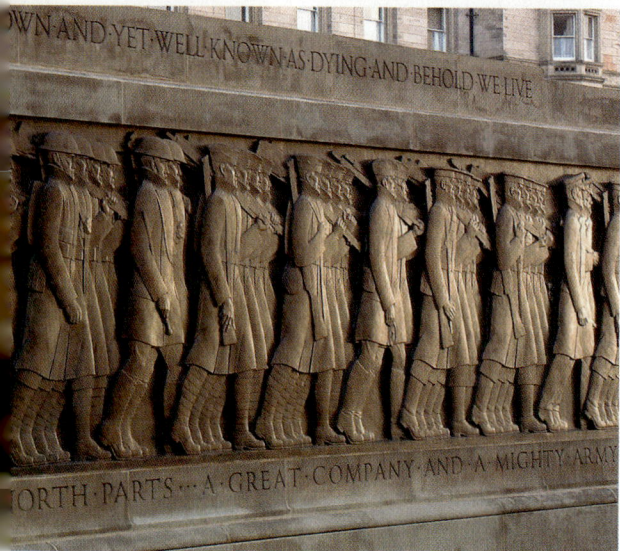

Cenotaph

■ Poignant and strikingly futurist at the same time, this was a collaboration between Lionel Budden, Professor of Architecture at Liverpool University, and H Tyson Smith, the city's foremost sculptor in the early 20th Century. Unveiled in 1930 to commemorate Liverpool's dead in the First World War, it features two 30ft bronze reliefs – one side with mourners in a cemetery, the other with soldiers marching in rank. The latter's inscription comes from the Book of Ezekiel: 'Out of the north parts...a great company and a mighty army'. A Second World War plaque was added in 1946.

Wellington Column

■ A Doric column erected 11 years
after the Duke's death in 1852,
with plaques of his victories and
a relief of Waterloo at the base.
Legend has it, his bronze statue
is cast from gun-metal salvaged
from the battle.

The birth of Liverpool, frame by frame

■ Along the east façade of St George's Hall, either side of the main entrance, are two sets of six reliefs sculpted by Thomas Stirling Lee, Charles Allen and Conrad Dressler between 1885 and 1901. The first, entitled The Progress of Justice (top row), is shown after cleaning in 2005; the second, National Prosperity, prior to its own restoration. The nude figures caused a scandal in their day.

1 Joy follows the growth of Justice, led by Conscience, directed by Wisdom

2 Justice, in her purity, refuses to be diverted by Wealth and Fame

3 Justice upholds the world, supported by Knowledge and Right

1 Liverpool, a municipality, employs labour and encourages art

2 Liverpool collects produce and exports, the manufactures of the country

3 Liverpool imports cattle and wool, for food and clothing

4 Justice, able to stand alone, administers by the sword

5 Justice, relieved of her sword by Virtue, and of her scales by Concord

6 Justice receives the kiss of Righteousness, and the crown of Immortality

4 Liverpool, by its imports, supplies the country with food and corn

5 Liverpool, by her shipwrights, builds vessels of commerce

6 Liverpool, a fishing village, gives her sons the boat and the net

Introducing...

Sapporo Teppanyaki

■ Sapporo Teppanyaki restaurant, sushi and noodle bar is Liverpool's only destination for Japanese cuisine (Upper Duke Street). Preparation of food is pure entertainment as expert Japanese chefs flaunt their outstanding skills and creative flair to ensure that every meal is a unique theatrical performance. In the spacious restaurant area, diners can enjoy the unique theatre of classic teppanyaki-style cooking with all the flames, noise and panache of this Japanese tradition.

Diners watch chefs prepare food while seated around their own dedicated grill station or 'teppan'. Tables range in size from 8 to 20, ideal for parties or special celebrations. The sushi and noodle bar is popular at lunchtime with guests looking for a lighter meal or healthy snack. Choose from an extensive range of freshly prepared sushi, sashimi and noodle dishes. Children are positively welcome. Visit our website at **sapporo.co.uk** for more details.

5.
Rope Walks

■ If it feels like you're in an urban village, it's because you are. A 24/7 tumult of activity, this historic area really was a ropery at the turn of the 19th Century, supplying the sailing ships of the age. Its vibe today comes from the feeling of flux when you wander up Bold Street, through the crowds and multi-lingual chatter, past the buskers, specialist stores and charismatic cafés and delis with their late Georgian and mock Florentine facades on a thoroughfare once compared with London's Bond Street, and hang a right through a warren of hard hats, drills and cranes to the artist studios of Duke Street and the beginning of Chinatown. It's a noisy, anarchic work in process, criss-crossed with squares, gardens and walkways, and blessed with 90 listed buildings and an embarrassment of bars and clubs.

Tea Factory

■ Formerly the premises of Mantunna, it's now a £10million, mixed-use scheme with Bluu Bar and the Tea Factory Bar & Kitchen based at ground-level and offices and plush penthouses on top. There's also gallery and exhibition space at CUBE (Centre for the Understanding of the Built Environment) and the northern offices of RIBA (Royal Institute of British Architects) next door. All linked by a new square to St Peter's on Fleet Street, the city's oldest church (founded in 1788 as a Benedictine mission).

FACT

■ Due east from the Tea Factory, the Foundation for Arts and Creative Technologies is the city's first purpose-built arts centre for more than 60 years, and very different in character to the surrounding red-brick warehouses. The emphasis is upon transparency and public access, with cantilevered stairs inside and glazed facades looking out across the cityscape. Throughout the building, the calm colours of natural materials provide a suitable backdrop for the art on display. Nice coffee, too.

Chinatown

■ The origins of Europe's oldest Chinatown, rolling down towards the south docks, lie in the Blue Funnel shipping line's routes between Liverpool and China from 1865. Six years later there were 200 Chinese people living in the city, and in 1886 Yee Chin's became its first Chinese laundry. Liverpool also has the country's first Chinese pub, The Nook, with beautiful fans above the doorways. Nelson Street remains the hub – where you'll still hear mah jong being played upstairs, the shuffle of tiles echoing through open windows like waves washed over pebbles. In the 1950s, no20 was home to the Liverpool Chinese Gospel Mission founded by Gladys Aylward. Her story was told in the movie The Inn of Sixth Happiness, starring Ingrid Bergman and children from Chinatown, and filmed in North Wales. The 15-metre Chinese Arch, a gift from sister-city Shanghai, is a blaze of gold, red and green, and adorned with 200 dragons. It marks a conduit down to the river according to the principles of feng shui.

LIVERPOOL'S FIRST AUTHENTIC
ITALIAN RESTAURANT

il forno
ITALIAN RESTAURANT

132 DUKE STREET
EAST VILLAGE
LIVERPOOL, L1 5AG
0151 709 4002

WWW.ILFORNO.CO.UK

RISTORANTE PIZZERIA DELICATESSEN PASTICCERIA GELATERIA

6.
Hope Quarter

■ On the brow of the big city sits a special place – a world of handsome Georgian properties, cobbled alleyways, awesome cathedrals and delightful pubs and restaurants. This was the address of Liverpool's most affluent citizens in the 19th Century, and today it's still a leafy retreat from the city-centre as well as a hotbed of arts, culture and academia, blending seamlessly into the main University campus. Take in the great views down to the Pier Head, and take time to explore the Hope Quarter's bucolic nooks and crannies. There is sweet music here...

6. Hope Quarter

The attractions...

- **GE** Central Hall
- **SA** St Andrew's Church
- **MC** Metropolitan Cathedral
- **ET** Everyman Theatre
- **PH** Philharmonic Hall
- **PN** St Philip Neri/ Spanish Garden
- **AC** Anglican Cathedral
- **SJ** St James Cemetery
- **LP** LIPA
- **CH** Chambre-Hardman House
- **UT** Unity Theatre
- **GB** Gladstone's Birthplace
- **SL** St Luke's Church
- **RS** Roman Standard

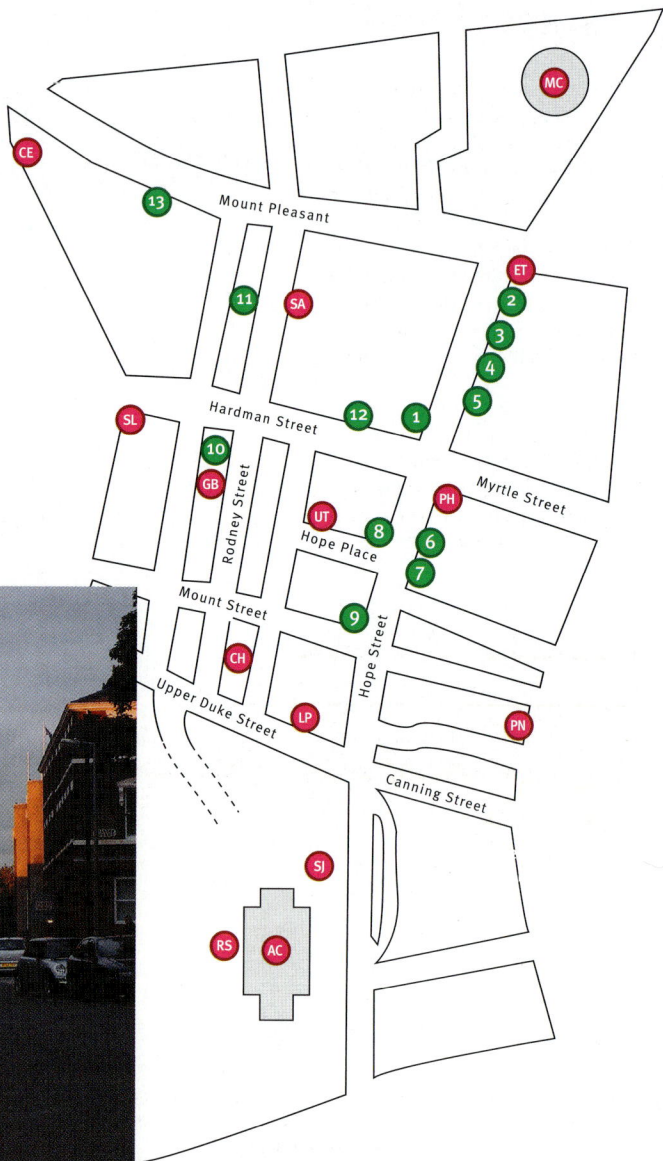

N

MC

CE

13 Mount Pleasant

ET

11 SA 2

3

4

SL Hardman Street 12 1 5

10 Myrtle Street

GB

UT PH

Hope Place 8 6

Rodney Street 7

Mount Street 9

CH Hope Street

Upper Duke Street LP PN

Canning Street

SJ

RS AC

Central Hall

■ On Renshaw Street so not technically Hope Quarter, but too grand to miss out. Today it hosts Rawhide comedy nights, but this was the original meeting-place of Liverpool's Unitarians, who had their roots in the non-conformist movement of the 17th Century (like Islam and Judaism believing God was one and Jesus a prophet to be followed rather than worshipped). They were a powerful, free-thinking influence in the city, counting philanthropist William Roscoe among their congregation (he's buried in the adjacent gardens named after him). In 1899 they moved their church to Ullet Road.

Quiet, now

The bars and restaurants...

1. Philharmonic Hotel
2. Everyman Bistro
3. Casa
4. El Macho
5. Other Place
6. Lower Place
7. Ego
8. London Carriage Works
9. 60 Hope Street
10. Valparaiso
11. Puschka
12. Magnet
13. Heart and Soul

St Luke's Church

■ Or the 'Bombed-out Church' as locals call it. Dominating the top of Bold Street, on the corner of Berry Street and Leece Street, it was completed in 1831 but damaged during the Second World War and now stands as a memorial to peace and place of tranquillity. There's a monument to Irish emigrants and the Great Famine near the entrance gates on Leece Street.

Philharmonic Hotel

■ Not so much a public house as a work of genius. Built in 1900 to the designs of Walter Thomas (not the Liver Building architect) with a little help from the University's School of Art, it features caryatids (sculptured female figures), plaster friezes, stained glass and splendid decoration throughout. Much of the joinery work was carried out by ship's carpenters used to working on the interiors of transatlantic liner. A public bar, grande lounge and snugs called Brahms and Liszt.

St Andrew's Church

■ The pyramid tomb in the Grade II listed graveyard of this Rodney Street church is thought to hold the body of railway engineer and infamous poker player William Mackenzie, sitting at a table holding a Royal Flush. According to legend, he sold his soul to the devil and believed that being laid to rest above ground would save him from damnation. Spooky.

Rodney Street

■ These days the Georgian terraces of Liverpool's Harley Street are home to physiotherapists, chiropodists, acupuncturists and dental surgeons. But they're also an historical Who's Who of the city. Ready for this? James Maury, the first US Consul in Liverpool, lived at no4 from 1790 to 1829. Nos9, 11, 34 and 62 were the respective birthplaces of poet Arthur Clough (friend of Longfellow and Thackeray), naval officer and author Nicholas Monsarrat (The Cruel Sea), Henry Booth (founder of the Liverpool & Manchester Railway) and William Gladstone (four times Prime Minister). Radiology pioneer C Thurston Holland worked at no43. William Duncan, Liverpool's first Medical Officer of Health, lived at no54. And Lytton Strachey, biographer and Bloomsbury Group confidante of Virginia Wolf, once occupied no80.

Chambre-Hardman House

■ At 59 Rodney Street, the time-capsule home and studio of photographer Edward Chambre-Hardman has been converted into an interactive museum by the National Trust with Heritage Lottery funding, and was opened to the public in 2004 following a preview exhibition at Central Library (called E Chambre-Hardman: Behind the Lens). He was born in Dublin and moved to Liverpool in the early 1920s, capturing liners sailing in and out of the port, the construction of the aircraft-carrier Ark Royal and superstars like Ivor Novello, Robert Donat and Margot Fonteyn at the Playhouse (for whom he was the official photographer). Twenty of his best-known works, along with the tools of his trade (including camera and 150,000 prints, negatives and glass plates), are now displayed in this restored 1940s interior.

Philharmonic Hall

■ It's been called 'frozen music' and it's that man Herbert Rowse again – this time fusing modernist style with acoustic data to design another landmark building (after the original hall's fire in 1933). He described it as "shaped like a megaphone with the orchestra at the narrow end." Inside, there are etched-glass decorations, gilded reliefs of Apollo and a memorial to the musicians of the Titanic. Rowse's initials, it's claimed, are woven into the sumptuous carpets.

It happened here...

■ In 1836 Charles Dickens gave a speech at the Mechanics Institute (now LIPA) in the first of 19 visits to Liverpool. He usually stayed at the Adelphi Hotel, sailed twice from the city to America, fell in love with a girl from Breck Road in Anfield, walked New Brighton's sands and gave public readings of his books at the Philharmonic Hall and St George's Hall (he once called Liverpool "the Copperfield stronghold"). Off Park Road, just south of the city-centre, is a row of streets called Pickwick, Dombey and Dorrit, crossed by Dickens Street.

Metropolitan Cathedral

■ 'Paddy's Wigwam' and one of the sights that makes Liverpool, so Liverpool. Frederick Gibberd's epitome of 1960s monumental concrete design was completed in 1967 and boasts the world's largest stained-glass window in its Lantern Tower, which itself weighs 2,000 tons. A new approach and ramp have been added to the main entrance, which has panels depicting the winged emblems of the Evangelists – the man of Matthew, lion of Mark, ox of Luke and eagle of John.

Anglican Cathedral

Feeling dizzy?

Frills and drills

■ You can't see Bede, David, Paul, Chad, Gilbert, Guthlac, Michael, Nicholas, Martin, Peter, Oswald, James and Emmanuel. But boy, an you can hear them. The 13 mighty bells – Emmanuel alone weighs four tons – of this colossal Cathedral possess the heaviest and highest ringing peal in the world.

Designed by Giles Gilbert Scott, a 23-year-old Roman Catholic, the Anglican was 100 years old on 19 July 2004 – although you could add another 250million years if you were being palaeontological about the local sandstone used.

Either way, at 101,000sq ft – almost twice the size of St Paul's in London – it's the fifth largest cathedral in the world (behind St Peter's in Rome, St John in New York, Nativity of Mary in Milan and Mary of the Chair in Seville).

The sheer, brooding bulk of the Cathedral occupies most visitors, but take a closer look at some of the details. Among the carvings around the outside, for example, are two goggled and gas mask-wearing gargoyles – one grappling with a pneumatic drill, the other riding an aeroplane. No one's quite sure what they're doing here, or indeed who created them.

As it stands, this magnificent building welcomes 350,000 visitors and worshippers a year, with many taking in the incredible views of the city from the top of the Tower (accessed by two lifts and 108 stairs) A new visitor centre and gallery is being planned, with a two-storey extension in traditional limestone that'll take the Cathedral into the 21st Century.

St James Cemetery

■ In the shadow of the Anglican Cathedral is the most romantic cemetery in England, declared full in 1936 after almost 58,000 internments. Originally a vast quarry accessed via ramps and subterranean walkways, it has an ancient spring and graffiti dating back to 1727 (see page 101) carved into the sandstone walls. Sons and daughters of Kentucky, South Carolina, New York, New Jersey, Massachusetts and Pennsylvania are all buried here, and there are countless memorials to those that perished at sea.

The headstones of Liverpool history

Roman Standard

■ Tracey Emin's first public piece of art is a 14ft high sculpture featuring a small starling-like bird atop a bronze pole symbolic of Liverpool's neo-classical architecture (hence the name). It stands in the grounds of the Anglican Cathedral outside the Oratory, a miniature Greek temple designed by Victorian architect John Foster, and was commissioned as part of the North West's art05 celebrations.

El Jardin della Nuestra Senora

Spanish Garden

■ In the grounds of St Philip Neri's Church on Catharine Street, and a labour of love for its old reverend in the early 1950s. He paid a visit to the rooftop garden at Barkers department store on London's Kensington High Street and decided to create his own paradise on the Blitz-scarred land adjacent to his church. Passion flowers, marble columns, a water nymph and (allegedly) a fragment of a pillar from Gladstone's old address on Rodney Street.

University of Liverpool

■ The original red-brick university, founded in 1881 and now (after a survey in Scientist magazine) one of the top 10 universities in the world ouside the US where leading scientists want to work. It's spawned eight Nobel Laureates, including Sir James Chadwick for discovery of the neutron in 1936. The coat of arms has an open book with the motto Fiat Lux, meaning 'Let There Be Light', between three silver Liver Birds.

Canning Street

■ Feel like you've just stepped back in time? This street, together with Percy Street, Huskisson Street, Falkner Square and Gambier Terrace, comprises a conservation area of supremely elegant late Georgian and Victorian housing with columned porches and grand balconies. Once home to Liverpool's gentry, it has a much younger population these days and is regularly commandeered by camera crews for period dramas (David Copperfield, Sherlock Holmes, Forsyte Saga etc).

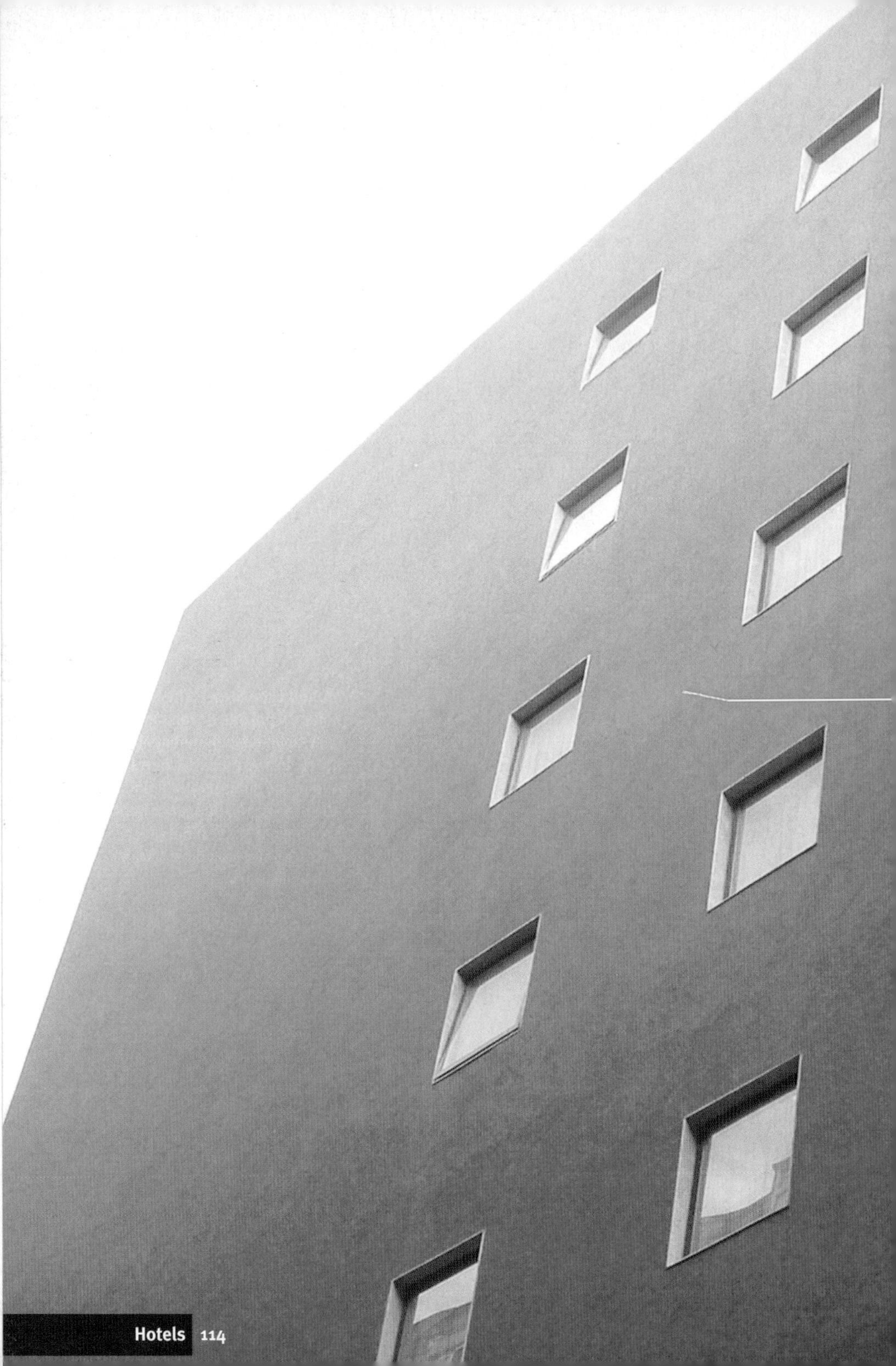

City centre

◼ Sir Thomas Hotel ★★★
24 Sir Thomas Street L1 6JB
Tel: (0151) 236 1366
Visit: sirthomashotel.co.uk
Currently the closest hotel to
Mathew Street (on the site of one
of the city's first banks) with a wine
bar (with a fab glass-encased wine
bin) and the St John restaurant
downstairs. The décor? is a mix of
contemporary furnishings, plush
velvet and tasteful marbles.

◼ Premier Travel Inn ★★★
Vernon Street L2 2AY
Tel: (0870) 238 3323
Visit: premiertravelinn.co.uk
A new arrival in the Business
(or recently renamed'Live/Work')
District of the city, linking
Tithebarn and Dale Street
and close to the Merseyrail
station at Moorfields.

◼ Travelodge ★★
25 Old Haymarket L1 6ER
Tel: 0870 191 1656
Visit: travelodge.co.uk
Bold and blue (main pic)
and designed with real character
by Urban Splash to the tune of
£5million. Next to the Queensway
tunnel entrance and a short walk
to William Brown Street.

◼ Marriott City Centre ★★★★
One Queen Square L1 1RH
Tel: (0151) 476 8000
Visit: marriott.com
Walk through Lime Street's sliding
doors and there she blows, one of
a high-density fusion of attractive,
modern buildings (housing Italian,
Chinese, Mexican and tapas
restaurants, plus a cocktail bar and
pub) that lie between the main
shopping district and the cultural
attractions of William Brown Street.
Its Olivier's restaurant is an award-
winner, and the Leisure Club has
a swimming pool and spa bath.

◼ Liner at Liverpool★★★
Lord Nelson Street L3 5QB
Tel: (0151) 709 7050
Formerly the Gladstone Hotel,
now completely refurbed into a
154-cabin hotel with décor inspired
by a luxury liner. Facilities include
conference and training rooms as
well as family accommodation.

◼ Holiday Inn ★★★
Lime Street L1 1NQ
Tel: (0151) 709 7090
Visit: holiday-inn.com
Recently refurbished with meeting
suites named after four of
Liverpool's twin cities: Shanghai,
Dublin, Cologne and New York.

◼ Adelphi Hotel ★★★
Ranelagh Place L3 5UL
Tel: (0151) 709 7200
Visit: britanniahotels.com
Almost 200 years old and a legend
in its own primetime as fans of the
BBC docusoap will recall. In its
early 20th Century heyday it was
one of the most luxurious hotels
in Europe and an arrival and
departure point for transatlantic
passengers (its Sefton Suite is a
replica of the First Class Smoking
Lounge on the Titanic). Today many
of the rooms still feature solid
marble walls and the original white
marble swimming pool has been
refurbished. A French restaurant,
carvery and choice of bars, plus
facilities for up to 800 guests,
all a short walk from Lime Street.

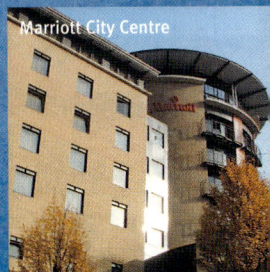
Marriott City Centre

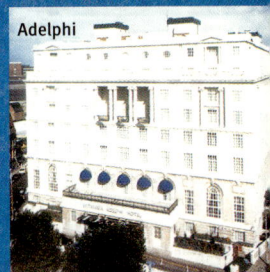
Adelphi

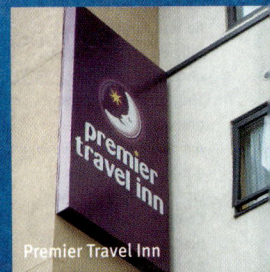
Premier Travel Inn

■ Ibis ★★/Express
27 Wapping, Baltic Triangle L1 8DQ
Tel: (0151) 706 9800
Visit: ibishotel.com
Next door to Formule 1. Prides itself
on solving problems in 15 minutes.

■ Premier Travel Inn ★★★
East Britannia Building,
Albert Dock L3 4AD
Tel: 0870 990 6432
Visit: premiertravelinn.com
A trusty stop-over for Albert Dock
tourists, opened in 2003 next door
to the Beatles Story museum.

■ Express by Holiday Inn ★★★/Express
Britannia Pavillion,
Albert Dock L3 4AD
Tel: (0151) 709 1133
Visit: hiexpress.com
Incorporated into the Dock's
existing structure. Handy for visits
to the plush Pan American Club.

■ Campanile ★★/Express
Queens Dock L3 4AJ
Tel: (0151) 709 8104
Visit: campanile.fr
At night its green neon glows next
to the Leo Casino's electric blue
and pink (also owned by Amaury
Taittinger, from the famous
French champagne dynasty).

■ Dolby ★★/Express
Queens Dock L3 4DE
Tel: (0151) 708 7272
Visit: dolbyhotels.co.uk
Just turned 10 years old, and
a favourite haunt for budget
travellers. Over 60 rooms with
satellite TV and ensuite shower.

■ Travelodge South ★★/Express
Brunswick Dock L3 4BH
Tel: 0870 191 1530.
Visit: travelodge.co.uk
By Harry Ramsden's with a great
view of the Marina and Graces.

Watch the birdies (and the fishies)...

■ Shock horror – you can still find hotels with that touch of individuality, not to mention the odd beautiful work of art and sculpture, in a big city like Liverpool. To truly appreciate Cormorants Diving (left), hanging in the lobby of the Thistle Hotel on Chapel Street, you have to visualise the ceiling level as the ocean surface with the birds diving through and disturbing shoals of fish. On the ceiling over at Trials on Castle Street

there's an exquisite Liver Bird (right) amid the rococco decorations, while the entrance to the Sir Thomas Hotel (on the street of the same name) has ornate lamps in the shape of orchids. Back on Chapel Street the huge canvas in the Racquet Club's famous Ziba restaurant, originally purchased at an auction in Antwerp, is a 19th-century copy of a medieval painting of the Medicis hunting. So now you know...

Suburbs

North

■ Royal Hotel ★★★
Marine Terrace, Waterloo L22 5PR
Tel: **(0151) 928 2332**
Visit: **liverpool-royalhotel.co.uk**
Perfect for Aintree or the football.
with a refurbished Seabank Lounge
with comfy leather chesterfields.

■ Suites Hotel ★★★★
**Ribblers Lane, Knowsley,
Prescot L34 9HA**
Tel: **(0151) 549 2222**
Presenting 80 rooms on four floors
in one of the best business and
banqueting venues in the North.

■ Devonshire House ★★★
293-297 Edge Lane L7 9LD
Tel: **(0151) 264 6600**
Visit: **devonshirehousehotel.com**
Georgian building in two acres
of gardens. A la carte restaurant
and conference rooms.

South

■ Marriott South ★★★★
**Speke Aerodrome,
Speke Road L24 8QD**
Tel: **(0151) 494 5050**
Visit: **marriott.com**
In the original Airport terminal
buildings with their Art Deco
interiors. Use of the David Lloyd
leisure centre and shuttle to JLA.

■ Woolton Redbourne ★★★★
Acrefield Road L25 5JN
Tel: **0845 601 1125**
Visit: **merseyworld.com/
woolton-redbourne**
Celeb-friendly venue with
a restaurant open to non-residents.
Originally a country house designed

by a Victorian industrialist, it's set
amid landscaped gardens with
rooms furnished in period style
and an imaginative table d'hôte.

■ Alicia Hotel ★★★
3 Aigburth Drive L17 3AA
Tel: **(0151) 727 4411**
Beautifully illuminated on the
boulevard encircling Sefton Park,
and top service around the clock.

■ Blenheim Lodge ★★★
**37 Aigburth Drive,
Sefton Park L17 4JE**
Tel: **(0151) 727 7380**
Spacious, privately-run guesthouse
on the Beatles trail as the former
digs of Stuart Sutcliffe.

■ Park Lane Hotel ★★★
23 Aigburth Drive L17 4JQ
Tel: **(0151) 727 4754**
Hotel dating back to the 18th
Century and tastefully refurbished.

■ Holme Leigh Guest House
93 Woodcroft Road, Wavertree L15
Tel: **(0151) 734 2216**
Just 2km from the city-centre,
a recently-refurbished Victorian
red-brick guest house, and always
a relaxing atmosphere.

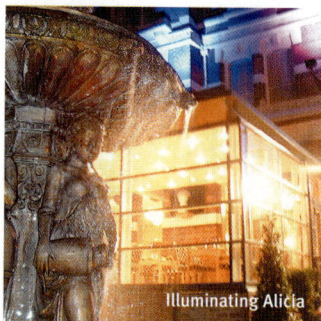

Illuminating Alicia

The young ones...

■ Liverpool's YHA
hostel (0870 770 5924)
is in its own secure
area on Wapping
(opposite Brunswick
Dock and not far from
Albert Dock) with the
historic Baltic Fleet
public house (check
out the Wapping brews
on tap), swinging
Blundell Street bar
and restaurant (for
those who like good
food with an authentic
Brat Pack tribute act
to follow) and a good
old-fashioned
McDonald's for
company. As usual
there's 24-hour access,
onsite parking (with
room for two coaches)
and all rooms are
ensuite (multi-share
for 3,4 or 6). By
general consent the
self-catering kitchen is
excellent, and there's
a café area for evening
meals plus a games
room and TV lounge
with Beatles décor
and usually a good
mix of world travellers.

Ready to order

The best cuisine in Liverpool. From around the world with love

The business and prix fixe menus at Colin's Bridewell, a gastropub in a converted police station in Rope Walks, say it all: Thai green curry; parmesan gratin tart with mizuna leaf; trout stuffed with Caribbean wild rice; and tortellini pasta with goat's cheese sauce. Whatever you want to eat you'll find it in a city whose variety of cuisine reflects its rich multi-cultural heritage. There are the aesthetics of dining out to consider, too. Choose modern British cooking in minimalist steel-and-glass venues on the waterfront, authentic Russian food in the raucous environs of Rope Walks, sophisticated international cuisine in the city's theatreland, and just about everything in-between. The following 40 restaurants represent a cross-section of what to expect. There are good modern venues at Queen Square (between the Shopping Centre and Cultural Quarter), a stretch of fabulous establishments in the Hope Quarter, and numerous lounge-bar options around the Business District and Albert Dock. And that's not including the dim-sum delights of Chinatown and abundance of cool cafés all over town. You're salivating, we can tell.

International

■ **3345 RW**
Parr Street Studios L1 4JN
Tel: (0151) 708 6345
They've fed stars from Gwyneth
Paltrow to Tracey Emin, and their
eclectic menu plunders the globe.
Inventive, quirky and sumptuous.

■ **Heart and Soul HQ**
62 Mount Pleasant L3 5SD
Tel: (0151) 707 9276
'Food, music and love' brought
to you in a beautifully restored
Georgian merchant's house.
Downstairs serves pizzas, pastas,
grills and tapas, upstairs has
seasonal specials and outside
there's a sun-trapping courtyard.
Funky house on Tuesday nights,
blue-note jazz on Wednesdays.

■ **London Carriage Works HQ**
40 Hope Street L2 9DA
Tel: (0151) 709 3000
Visit: hopestreethotel.co.uk
On the ground floor of the Hope
Street Hotel and aiming for Michelin
star status by 2008 – something
both the Sunday Times and
Decanter think they can achieve.
We're no white wine connoisseurs,
but hey – if those Fleurs d'Alsace
take some beating. As do the
seafood dishes created by chef Paul
Askew. If we had the shrapnel we'd
be up here every night.

■ **Tea Factory Bar & Kitchen RW**
Fleet Street (next to FACT) L1 4DQ
Tel: (0151) 708 7008
Relaxed environment with an eye-
catching mural depicting Liverpool's
historic trade routes – a theme
repeated in the 'global tapas' at
the bar. The mezzanine restaurant
has a 'theatre' of an open kitchen.

Location key:

PH Pier Head/Albert Dock
BD Business District
SC Shopping Centre
CQ Cultural Quarter
RW Rope Walks
HQ Hope Quarter

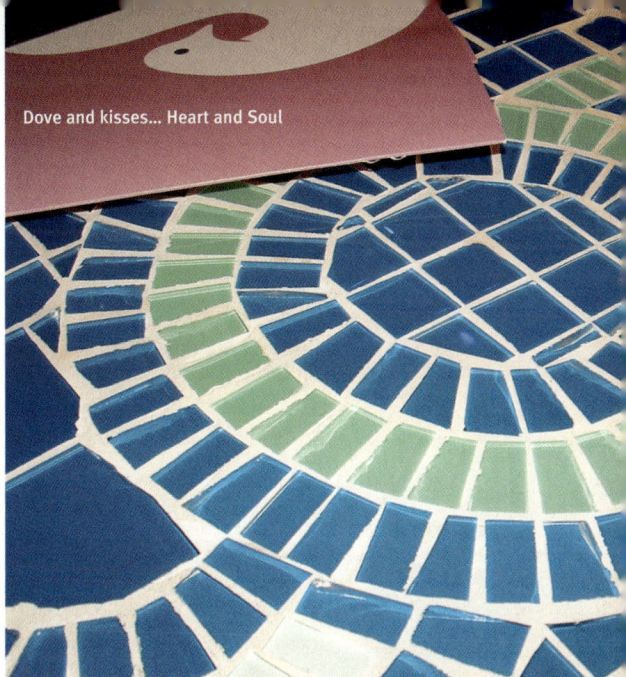
Dove and kisses... Heart and Soul

European

■ **60 Hope Street HQ**
60 Hope Street L1 9BZ
Tel: (0151) 707 6060
Visit: 60hopestreet.com
A destination restaurant in the truest sense, and also becoming something of an international art gallery. From Time Out London: 'Tasteful and tranquil, the emphasis is on classy, creative cooking in a discreet, arty but unstuffy setting... From the outside, the place looks severe, but they serve a deep-fried jam sandwich and give you an Uncle Joe's mint ball as you leave'.

■ **Albany Dining Rooms BD**
2 Ormond Street L3 9RQ
Tel: (0151) 242 1659
Visit: albanydiningrooms.co.uk
Just opened and housed in a restored gem. The brasserie is the brainchild of a restauranteur whose previous projects include the Longrain in Sydney and London's Voodoo Lounge. Pan-European cuisine with views of the central courtyard and garden.

■ **Ego HQ**
57 Hope Street L1 9BW
Tel: (0151) 706 0707
Visit: egorestaurants.com
A seasonal menu based on 'rustic Mediterranean cuisine' sourced from the region. Sunny side up.

■ **The Lower Place HQ**
Philharmonic Hall,
Hope Street L1 9BP
Tel: (0151) 210 1955
Good Food Guide-listed, with tapas nights to coincide with performances upstairs at the Phil.

British

Swish at St John's

■ **Simply Heathcotes BD**
Beetham Plaza,
25 The Strand L2 0XL
Tel: (0151) 236 3536
Visit: heathcotes.co.uk
Modern British cuisine at its best from Paul Heathcote, with special offers on Monday nights featuring a choice of selected a la carte dishes.

■ **Ziba @ The Racquet Club BD**
5 Chapel Street L3 9AG
Tel: (0151) 236 6676
Visit: racquetclub.co.uk
Located in Liverpool's premier boutique hotel, with a former Conran cook as head chef. Cool.

■ **St John's Restaurant & Bar BD**
24 Sir Thomas Street L1 6LB
Tel: (0151) 236 1366
Downstairs at the Sir Thomas Hotel. 'Steaks sourced from young steers fetted on the lush, green grass of Curwin Hill', and Mrs Kirkham's Smoked Lancashire Cheese.

Bistros

■ **Everyman Bistro HQ**
Everyman Theatre,
9-11 Hope Street L1 9BH
Tel: (0151) 708 9545
Visit: everyman.co.uk
A regular in food and wine guides
and the only venue to receive an
A* in the Observer/Harden guide
for great value and atmosphere.

■ **Pierre Victoire SC**
14 Button Street L2 6PS
Tel: (0151) 227 2577
The little corner of Liverpool that's
forever Paris, in a converted
warehouse just around the corner
from Ted Baker in the Cavern
Quarter. Mussels in white wine
are a speciality.

Vive La Victoire

■ **Puschka HQ**
16 Rodney Street L1 2TE
Tel: (0151) 708 8698
Outstanding example of How
To Get It Right. And participating
in the 2004 Liverpool Biennial
with an 'Art in the Bar' exhibition.

■ **The Other Place HQ**
29A Hope Street L1 9BQ
Tel: (0151) 707 7888
Intimate little eaterie on the same
block as the Everyman and Casa.

Hotels

■ **The Brasserie @ Crowne Plaza PH**
2 St Nicholas Place,
Princes Dock L3 1QW
Tel: (0151) 243 8000
Visit: cpliverpool.com
Contemporary international dishes
from the one of the city's poshest
hotels. And a great breakfast.

■ **Filini @ Radisson SAS PH**
107 Old Hall Street L3 9BD
Tel: (0151) 966 1500
Visit: radissonsas.com
Inspired by the best of Sardinian
cuisine, with an exclusively Italian
wine list and arguably the best river
view of any Liverpool restaurant.

■ **Olivier's @ Marriott City SC**
Queen Square L1 1RH
Tel: (0151) 476 8000
Visit: marriott.com
You can tell it's somewhere swanky
when Sir Larry's plastered all over
the walls and the menu has
'To Commence' at the top. But
there's 'traditional Scouse' as well
as sautéed chicken livers to choose from.

Where to get great...

- Crispy duck with honey roasted apples .... **Piccolino**
- Monkfish with lemon dressing and baby fennel .... **Heart and Soul**
- Seafood paella with black tiger prawns and squid .... **La Vina**
- Grilled polenta topped with sauteed artichoke .... **Courtyard**
- Fried sliced pork with capsicum and blackbean sauce .... **Mei Mei**
- Chargrilled burger with ciabatta and garlic mayonnaise .... **Olive Press**
- Plump Cumberland sausage and fluffy mash .... **Slaughterhouse**
- Ballotine of foie gras with brioche and mead ..... **Ziba @ Racquet Club**
- Thai red curry chicken with coconut milk .... **Orchid Spring**
- Roasted red pepper risotto with spinach and truffle ...... **St Petersburg**
- Butternut squash ravioli with nutmeg foam ...... **Filini @ Radisson SAS**
- Calzone with mozzarella and chopped ham .... **Al Andalus**

Lovely show, Lovely time x Mrs G, Liverpool

Wonderful food Miss J, Germany

Such a **theatrical** night! Mr M, Stoke

A superb **japanese** restaurant!

Cool **cuisine**, thank you! Mr D, Chester

A perfect end to my trip! Mrs G, Sheffield

Best service, Unbelievable Mr C, Stoke

So fresh and stylish Mrs P, Liverpool

What an experience! Mr & Mrs F, Liverpool

What an anniversary! Mr & Mrs H, London

Fantastic! Ms C, Wales Excellent! Mr B, Southport

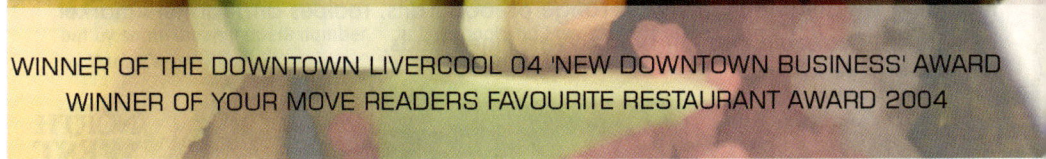

WINNER OF THE DOWNTOWN LIVERCOOL 04 'NEW DOWNTOWN BUSINESS' AWARD
WINNER OF YOUR MOVE READERS FAVOURITE RESTAURANT AWARD 2004

Sapporo Teppanyaki
134 Duke Street
East Village
Liverpool
L1 5AG
T: 0151 705 3005

Sapporo
Teppanyaki
restaurant

sushi & noodle bar

Italian

■ **ASK SC**
Queen Square L1 1FS
Tel: (0151) 709 0080
Local branch of Adam and Sam
Kaye's reliable restaurant chain.

■ **Casa Italia BD**
40 Stanley Street L1 6AL
Tel: (0151) 227 5774
Family-run fixture for 25 years,
and an award-winning trattoria.

■ **Est Est Est PH**
Albert Dock L3 4AF
Tel: (0151) 408 6969
Delicious dilemmas in the light,
bright Albert Dock favourite.

■ **Franco's @ Bar Italia BD**
48A Castle Street L2 2LQ
Tel: (0151) 236 3375
Try the gamberoni alla Franco – the
chef's king prawn secret recipe.

■ **Il Forno RW**
132 Duke Street L1 5AG
Tel: (0151) 709 4002
Opened in May 2005 as 'Liverpool's
first authentic Italian restaurant'.

■ **Olive Press Pizzeria BD**
25-27 Castle Street L2 4TA
Tel: (0151) 227 2242
Live Canadian lobsters, Peroni on
draught, hand-made artisan pasta.

■ **Piccolino BD**
14A Cook Street L2 9QU
Tel: (0151) 236 2555
'Always individual, consistently
excellent'. Live jazz every Sunday.

■ **Villa Romana RW**
6-8 Wood Street L1 4AQ
Tel: (0151) 708 8004
Local fave. Legendary antipasti.

Take your Piccolino

Olive Press in action

South Asian

■ **Shere Khan RW**
17-19 Berry Street L1 4SD
Tel: (0151) 709 6099
One of a chain of seven curry houses owned by millionaire restauranteur Nighat Awan and marketing itself as 'the McDonald's of Indian food'. Modern decor, and you can purchase sauces and pickles for sale at the counter.

■ **Sultan's Palace BD**
75-77 Victoria Street L2 6TN
Tel: (0151) 227 9020
Opulent basement restaurant with chefs poached from five-star hotels in Delhi to create the very best Indian food. Low-fat, healthy dishes prepared in a tandoor oven. The fish kofta comes highly recommended.

Enter the dragon

■ At the last count there were 18 restaurants in Liverpool's Chinatown (in Rope Walks), most of them on Nelson Street with a few on nearby Berry Street. Of course, there are other great Chinese venues outside the district, notably Chung Ku on Riverside Drive (vaunted in The Good Food Guide for its excellent dim sum range), Tai Pan on Great Howard Street (one of the Observer Food Monthly magazine's top five Chinese restaurants in the country) and May Sum in St John's Precinct (Liverpool's biggest eat-as-much-as-you-like buffet restaurant). And back in Chinatown two great supermarkets to explore: Hondo on Upper Duke Street (by Yuet Ben), and Chung Wah on the corner of Hardy Street and St James Street.

South East Asian

■ **Mayflower RW**
48 Duke Street L1 5AS
Tel: (0151) 709 6339
Visit: index.force9.co.uk/mayflower
Dishes from Peking, Canton and Szechuan, with two floors and a private suite for parties and functions. And just look at the size of those banquets.

■ **Mei Mei RW**
9-13 Berry Street L1 9DF
Tel: (0151) 707 2888
A new arrival with just the best range of banquets (Royal, Vegetarian, Noble etc). Constantly frequented by Chinese customers, which is always a good sign.

■ **Orchid Spring SC**
47 Paradise Street L1 3BP
Tel: (0151) 708 8400
A shangri-la of Thai cuisine on Paradise Street, one down from Radio Merseyside, and a big hit with clock-watching office workers at lunchtime. Who says tapas has to be Spanish? A typical Thai meal consists of hot, spicy, sweet and sour dishes that'll have you hooked.

■ **Sapporo Teppanyaki RW**
134 Duke Street L1 5AG
Tel: (0151) 705 3005
Visit: sapporoteppanyaki.com
Sushi and noodle café-bar opened in 2003 as Liverpool's entry-point into Japanese dining. A chef is assigned to each table as diners watch their food being prepared.

■ **Yuet Ben RW**
1 Upper Duke Street L1 9DU
Tel: (0151) 709 5772
A fixture for 35 years and favourite among discerning lovers of Chinese food. Self-styled as 'Liverpool's original Peking-style restaurant'. Yuet Ben means 'Honoured Guest'.

More, more at Mei Mei

Theatre chefs, Sapporo

Iberian

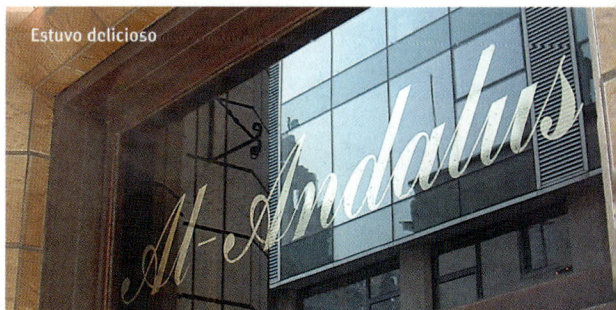
Estuvo delicioso

■ **Al Andalus BD**
2 Brunswick Street L2 0PL
Tel: (0151) 236 0137
One of 10 Spanish restaurants
in the UK recommended by the
Guardian who say, 'If you and
your friends want to enjoy Spanish
cooking at its finest, this is the
place to come'.

■ **Algarve BD**
20 Stanley Street L1 6AF
Tel: (0151) 236 0206
Visit: algarverestaurant.co.uk
Authentic Portuguese restaurant
with a special banquet offer
featuring sardines, omelette, grilled
lamb chop, chicken piri, fried crab
claws, mussels, mushrooms and
garlic bread. And an espresso!

■ **Don Pepe BD**
19-21 Victoria Street L1 6BD
Tel: (0151) 231 1909
The succulent steak and rich
vegetarian paella options give this
well-established place the classy
reputation it deserves. Dig the
huge central fountain.

■ **La Tasca SC**
3 Queen Square L1 1RH
Tel: (0151) 709 1070
Big, lively tapas bar behind the
Marriott Hotel. Most of the staff
are Spanish, and the dishes are
traditional and tasty.

■ **La Vina BD**
11-15 North John Street L2 5QY
Tel: (0151) 255 1401
Four Spaniards in charge of a
Spanish restaurant serving up
dishes with a Galician twist and
exclusive wine like the King of
Spain's fave, Vega-Sicilia Cosecha.

Americas

■ **El Macho HQ**
23 Hope Street L1 9BQ
Tel: (0151) 708 6644
Visit: elmachorestaurants.co.uk
Opened in 1985 by two brothers
from Baja. Well-known for its
pueblo-style interior, great
atmosphere and fantastic skillets
and charcoal-grilled steaks.

■ **Pan American Club PH**
22 Britannia Pavilion,
Albert Dock L3 4EF
Tel: (0151) 709 7097
Visit: lyceumgroup.co.uk/panamerican
Award-winning interior housed
in the old This Morning studios.
Traditional American cuisine
presented with the panache
of a Parisian brasserie.

■ **Valparaiso HQ**
4 Hardman Street L1 9AX
Tel: (0151) 708 6036
Visit: valparaiso-restaurant.co.uk
Minced beef topped with sweetcorn
or seafood paella with saffron rice?
The menu at Liverpool's only
Chilean restaurant, established
back in 1985, presents you with
delicious dilemmas. Owner Julio
Ernesto Arellano has some ripping
yarns to tell, too...

Chops away

Team La Vina

Propping up the bar at St Petersburg

North end...

■ **Charlie Parker's** (0151 928 1101) on Waterloo's Crosby Road North has earned a word-of-mouth reputation for its welcoming atmosphere and legendary Thai fishcakes. On nearby Church Road there's **Touchwood Bar** (0151 928 5656), a lounge venue that serves 'peewack', a traditional Scouse soup made of lentils and bacon ribs, and hosts salsa nights. As does **The Eating Room** (01704 873835) at Shorrocks Hill Country Club on Formby's Lifeboat Road. It's an international restaurant in a beautiful hotel and health club complex used by current and former top footballers.

South end...

■ Lark Lane in Aigburth is a bohemian outpost bursting with good restaurants. **Maranto's** (0151 727 7200) is admired for its American steak dishes, while at French bistro **L'Alouette** (0151 707 2837) tables by the open fire should be booked but the candlelit cosiness comes for free. **Que Pasa Cantina** (0151 727 0006) serves burritos, fajitas and lashings of Mexican beer, and **Esteban** (0151 727 6056) is a busy tapas bar. There's an open kitchen at Greek restaurant **Romio's** (0151 727 7252), global fusion at **Viva** (0151 726 0160) and elegant homeliness about **Keith's Wine Bar** (0151 728 7688). All down the one street.

Nearby Aigburth Road boasts **Gulshan** (0151 427 2273), recognised by the Michelin Guide and listed as one of the top 50 curry houses in the country by The Independent, while Allerton Road has the seafood speciliaties of **Fusion** (0151 724 6070), international tapas of **Pod** (0151 724 2255) and Vietnamese delights of **Fung Lok** (0151 722 9560). Towards town along Smithdown Road there's modern British cooking at **Jalons Wine Bar** (0151 734 0329), more global fusion at **Mustard** (0151 222 2466) and Thai delights at **Siam Garden** (0151 734 1471).

Russian

■ **St Petersburg** RW
7A York Street L1 5BN
Tel: (0151) 709 6676
A dozen types of blini on the menu, as well as home-made soups, caviar and beluga. Dishes from all 15 former Soviet republics and a pervasive French influence, too.

Turkish

■ **New Euro Palace** RW
94A Bold Street L1 4HY
Tel: (0151) 708 0806
Belly dancing, live music, great Turkish cuisine, and posh cocktail nights on Wednesdays.

Greek

■ **Christakis Taverna** RW
7 York Street L1 5BN
Tel: (0151) 708 7377
Visit: christakisgreektaverna.com
Beautiful building, countless courses, generous helpings, lots of dancing and plate smashing.

■ **Bellapais Cyprus Taverna** BD
Bixteth Street L3 9SG
Tel: (0151) 236 1881
Hot seafood specialities, gorgeous charcoal grills and sizzling Cypriot meals and casseroles to go round.

■ **Athina** RW
Hanover Street L1 4LN
Tel: (0151) 707 1557
In Gostins Building, with a local-born head chef who once worked at a plush two Michelin-starred restaurant in Berkshire.

All bar none

■ Where's the action? Depends what you're after. Down on the Albert Dock you'll find some of Liverpool's hippest bars. Further south, the high-rolling Leo Casino and Rat Pack-tastic Blundell Street.

Let's go the other way, across The Strand to Cooper's 'Good Time' Emporium. We're in the Business District now. Victoria Street is one long stretch of smart lounge-bars, plus some lovely pubs to rest those tired feet over a slow drink.

Between here and the Shopping Centre is Mathew Street, mad at weekends. It's a short walk to Queen Square, more of a foodie destination but with Yates's and The Rat & Parrot facing each other across the bus lane like two book-ends of bacchanalia. On to the Cultural Quarter and up Lime Street for some classic gin palaces.

Rope Walks rocks. Concert Square throbs with jeans-and-T-shirt bars and nearby Slater Street is Soho with a Scouse twist.

Up the hill, the Hope Quarter will bring out the bohemian in you. Student, stage-manager or secretary, you'll get that Greenwich Village feeling as the sun goes down – and often see famous faces fresh from performing at the Phil.

The following is just a sample. No space to mention the speed-dating, sports bars, Scouse House and hip-hop scene – you'll have to check the posters and flyers (KooKoo, Lemon Lounge, Chibuku, Circus etc) as you sally forth.

You're in clubbing paradise. Unless you fancy a quiet pint. Same again?

Pier Head and Albert Dock

Blue Bar: the height of chill

Baby Cream
Atlantic Pavilion,
Albert Dock L3 4AE
Tel: (0151) 707 1004
Visit: babycream.co.uk
From the people that gave us
global clubbing brand Cream and
legendary Liverpool lounge Blue.
The two best nights are Thursday,
when alternative dance collective
Ladytron play everything from
Nancy Sinatra to The Fall, and
Sunday, when Suncream's ambient
sounds kick in. If you like the
tracks, you can burn them onto a
CD there and then – courtesy of
the Creamselector touch-screen
digital music dispenser. What will
they think of next?

Baltic Fleet
33A Wapping L1 8DQ
Tel: (0151) 709 3116
Talk about a contrast. This is your
traditional (and very tourist-
friendly) dockside alehouse, with
authentic nautical memorabilia and
the kind of bevvies that put hair on
a stevedore's wellies. A quick one,
just to settle the dust...

Blue Bar & Grill
Edwards Pavilion,
Albert Dock L3 4AF
Tel: (0151) 709 7097
Visit: lyceumgroup.co.uk/bluebar
For Blue, read bling. Lots of it. The
deejay session du jour is Sunday's
Babylicious in Baby Blue, the
private members lounge. Just tell
them you know Felix Da Housecat.

Pan American Club
Britannia Pavilion,
Albert Dock L3 4AD
Tel: (0151) 702 5849
Visit: lyceumgroup.co.uk/panamerican
Gwyneth Paltrow tippled in this
immaculate sanctum recently
(probably not a brown-over-mild)
when hubbie Chris Martin was
recording with Coldplay at Parr
Street (see 3345 on page 149).

It's Baltic, out there

Garlands girls

Business District

Anderson's Bar
26 Exchange Street East L2 3PH
Tel: **(0151) 243 1330**
One-time piano bar that was
re-furbed at the end of 2002.
Very busy at lunchtimes and a fave
with post-work professionals.

Garlands
8-10 Eberle Street L2 2AG
Tel: **(0151) 236 3307**
Mardi Gras and Rio Carnival rolled
into one super-kitsch disco.
It celebrated its 10th birthday
with a card from Liza Minelli, after
whose mum it takes its name.

Late Lounge
3 Victoria Street L2 5QA
Tel: **(0151) 236 4832**
Between Metro and The Marquee,
a big and beautiful lounge with
pumping Scouse House on Sunday.

Living Room
15 Victoria Street
Tel: **(0151) 236 1999**
Visit: **livingroom.co.uk**
Arguably the classiest honky-tonk
in town – dig that grand piano –
and the brainchild of Tim Bacon,
MD of Living Ventures, whose
bold vision was to create "an
environment that caters for a broad
mix of people, I love the idea of a
place for everyone." Result: a cool,
airy interior with colonial browns
and creams and 150 cocktails.

Ma Boyle's
Tower Gardens,
Tower Buildings L3 1AB
Tel: **(0151) 236 1717**
Cosy downstairs gem at the back of
the redeveloped Tower Buildings.
Cracking seafood platters, great
maritime copper murals.

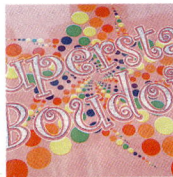

Carry on camping...

Liverpool's gay
quarter, located in and
around Stanley Street
(Business District) is
enjoying its own
renaissance. Popular
pubs include the
Lisbon, Pacos, G-Bar
and the Navy. Nearby
Superstar Boudoir is
the busiest gay bar in
town with 1,000
customers from all
over the North
West at weekends,
while Addiction on
Cumberland Street,
hosts KoOkoO ('Rum,
Bum & Concertina')
on the last Saturday
of the month and
Octopus (cabaret with
top local and national
acts) twice-monthly.
Garlands and its gay
and mixed crowd is
now back home on
Eberle Street. For
all the latest, visit
gayliverpool.com.

This is the Newz

Wheels of steel...

■ Where to start with Liverpool's throbbing club scene? Chibuku are four JMU graduates (named after a beer from Malawi) who started a monthly night at the Lemon Lounge on Berry Street, expanded to the Masque on Seel Street and are now regarded as one of the best underground nights in the country, attracting high-profile producers and deejays from LA to Ibiza. Over at Society on Duke Street, Friday resident Mike Da Scale is generally regarded as producing the best house in Liverpool right now, while Yousef is an internationally-acclaimed Liverpudlian deejay of Egyptian descent whose Circus night at the Masque was named Radio One's Club of the Year in 2005. For R&B, head for Concert Square at weekends and City FM deejay Spykatcha.

■ Marquee
**9 Fowler Buildings,
Victoria Street L2**
Tel: **(0151) 227 2127**
Visit: **marqueeukltd.co.uk**
Lounge bar and restaurant run by a Lebanese lecturer and Jordanian-Palestinian accountant, old friends in Liverpool for 20 years. Also starring a Syrian chef and solid RnB night on Sunday, brought to you by local radio deejay and London exile, Spykatcha.

■ Metro Eating Room & Bar
**5-9 Fowlers Building,
Victoria Street L2 5QA**
Tel: **(0151) 236 2200**
Just turned three in summer 2005, a lounge venue with a saloon-type bar and exposed-brick interior reminiscent of all those dockside warehouses.

■ Newz Bar
**New Zealand House,
18 Water Street L2 0TD**
Tel: **(0151) 236 2025**
Visit: newzbrasserie.com
One of the joints in which to be seen, so get glammed up and prepare to queue at weekends. Suit sans neckwear for the gentlemen, little black dresses for the ladies.

■ Pacific Bar & Grill
**Pacific Chambers,
11 Temple Street L2 5RH**
Tel: **(0151) 236 0270**
Visit: **pacificbarandgrill.com**
Multi TV screens behind the bar, a great selection of champagne (and Smirnoff Norsk) and lots of little corners to lounge and linger, not least the VIP Red Room. Plus a new menu introduced by former chefs at the Marriott Hotel.

Pig & Whistle
Covent Garden L2 8UA
Tel: **(0151) 236 4760**
Historic spit 'n' sawdust tavern by
the Racquet Club and Thistle Hotel.
'Emigrants supplied' is still visible
on an ancient brass plate.

Aldo's Place
38-40 Victoria Street L1 6BX
Tel: **(0151) 255 1252**
Opened by ex-Liverpool footballer
John Aldridge, with an Asian Fusion
restaurant called Thyme upstairs.

Rigby's
23-25 Dale Street L2 2EZ
Tel: **(0151) 236 3269**
It was founded in 1726. It used
to be called The George. It's got
a back-room that recalls the low-
beamed ceiling of a ship. And it's
packed with Horatio Nelson
memorabilia. Admiral stuff.

Ship & Mitre
133 Dale Street
Tel: **(0151) 236 0859**
Visit: **shipandmitre.co.uk**
Like your cask-conditioned ales?
Love this superb freehouse. Art
Deco exterior, and inside deliveries
every week from Germany, Belgium
and the Czech Republic – often just
one barrel of a particular brew.

The White Bar @ Radisson SAS
107 Old Hall Street L3 9BD
Tel: **(0151) 966 1500**
Visit: **radissonsas.com**
Plush watering-hole at posh new
hotel. They've kept the original
fisherman's cottages on the
outside and concocted some
adorable Martinis behind the bar.
Big plasma TV, bigger white piano.

Keeping it real…

■ Some cracking real ale pubs to sample. The Ship & Mitre (page 149) is royalty, while the Baltic Fleet (page 146) is famous for its range of Wapping beers. On Moorfields, the Lion Tavern is one of Robert Cain's Victorian gems – don't miss its daily cheese board! Up in Rope Walks, real-ale fans with a taste for heavy rock should head for the Swan Inn on Wood Street, with Jekyll's Gold and Belgian beers. In Hope Quarter, there's a traditional pub to 'enjoy a nice pint with no distracting music'. Called the Roscoe Head (on Roscoe Street, as it goes) it serves Tetley's Bitter and Mild, Jennings Ale plus two guest brews every week. Oh, and a great quiz on Tuesdays, and cribbage on Wednesdays.

Hope Quarter

**Best of 3...
party venues**

Royal Daffodil.
Cruising Mersey ferry
with two saloons,
a top sound system
and room for over
250 revellers
(0151 330 1458).

Palm House. Up to
400 people can party
beneath the majestic
glass canopy of Sefton
Park's Grade II
listed wonder
(0151 726 9304).

City Exchange
Atrium. A glass palace
in the Post & Echo
building (Business
District) with an open-
plan mezzanine
(0151 472 2805).

Blackburne Arms
24 Catharine Street L8 7NL
Tel: **(0151) 708 0252**
A congenial establishment in which
to feel at ease discussing Calasso's
treatise on the origins of Western
self-consciousness, or Carragher's
propensity to blow snot through
his nostril when he's knackered.

The Casa
29 Hope Street L1 9BQ
Tel: **(0151) 709 2148**
Small-but-perfectly-formed bar
that also functions as a creative
arts outlet for the dockers
community in the city and has a
great-value bistro-café downstairs.
A former writer in residence here
was Nicholas Allt, author of just-
published The Boys from The
Mersey (see page 215).

The Magnet
39-45 Hardman Street L1 9AS
Tel: **(0151) 709 6969**
Aptly-named – it draws punters
like moths to a flame from
Thursday onwards. A packed
bar upstairs and pre-meditated
mayhem in the labyrinthine
basement. You should try it.
We think you'll like it.

Peter Kavanagh's
2-6 Little Egerton Street L8 7LY
Tel: **(0151) 709 3443**
Much-loved public house that
reached the grand old age of 100
not out in 1997, and it's got the
Victorian décor to prove it. It was
named after a charismatic local
designer – those are his tables
in the snug – and adorned with
murals of scenes from Dickens
and Hogarth.

The Philharmonic Hotel
36 Hope Street L1 9BX
Tel: **(0151) 707 2837**
So good we've mentioned it twice
(see page 104). Proper name, the
Philharmonic Dining Rooms. Just
say the Phil – everyone'll know
where you mean. World famous,
and what a place to meet as a
starting-point for the evening.

The Pilgrim
34 Pilgrim Street L1 9HB
Tel: **(0151) 709 2302**
You go downstairs. You see lots of
LIPA students and Beatles pictures
on the walls. You say hello to Joe,
the hospitable proprietor. You have
a pint or three. You break into
something from the White Album.
You draw a tremendous burst
of silence. You did your best
and that's all that counts.

The Residents Lounge
**Hope Street Hotel,
40 Hope Street L1 9DA**
Tel: **(0151) 709 3000**
Underneath the restaurant and
boutique hotel, into a chilled
environment with live music on
Friday nights and beautiful people
everywhere you look. Chin chin.

Roscoe Head
24-26 Roscoe Street L1 2SX
Tel: **(0151) 709 4365**
Only 21 pubs in Britain have
featured in every copy of the
CAMRA Good Beer Guide since
1974. You're propping up the bar
in one of them. It's only diddy, but
who said size matters? Named after
one of Liverpool's philanthropists,
many of whose possessions are
displayed over in Central Library.

Hope Street Hotel: downstairs here
for the chilled-out Residents Lounge

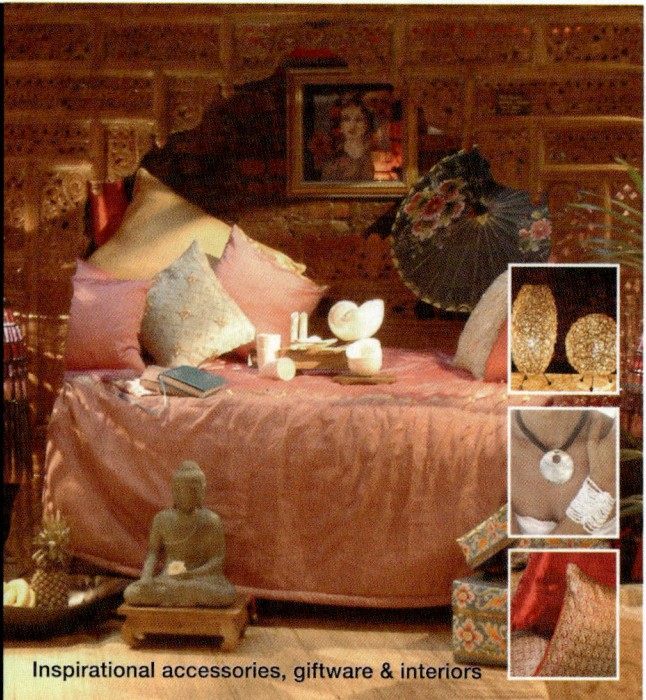

Big spenders

Haute couture or urbanwear? Whatever your passion in fashion, you'll find it here. Let's shop...

How can you tell that you're shopping in Liverpool? The streets are packed, there's a lavish helping of style and fashion stores, and somewhere a lonesome trumpeter is playing From Russia With Love.

Albert Dock has some fabulous furnishings and homeware shops, but the main drag is Church Street with the Cavern Walks and Clayton Square malls at either end.

All the big department and chain stores are present (Body Shop, Boots, Burtons, Dorothy Perkins, Gap, HMV, John Lewis, Karen Millen, Littlewoods, Marks and Spencer, Next, Top Shop, Virgin Megastore, WH Smith). But it's the unique boutiques and independents that'll really float your boat, becoming more quirky the further you venture up Bold Street (where the Shopping Centre blends into Rope Walks) and along super-eclectic Renshaw Street.

With the Met Quarter (Armani, Hugo Boss and Flannels) opening on Whitechapel and a multi-million-pound arcadia set for Paradise Street, shoppers are only going to be spoilt for more choice over the next few years. Goodness, how on earth will we all cope?

Feline feminine, with Arrogant Cat

Fashion

■ **10A SC**
Cavern Walks,
Mathew Street L2 6RE
Tel: (0151) 236 9400
A new store, opened by the owners of Giancarlo Ricci on Bold Street, with luxury labels like Versace Classic and Jeans Couture, and Dolce & Gabbana.

■ **Arrogant Cat SC**
1 Cavern Walks,
Mathew Street L2 6RE
Tel: (0151) 236 6001
Visit: arrogantcat.com
Sexy red-and-black decor and clothes unlike anything else in the city – courtesy of Somi Han, a graduate of Central St Martin's School of Art and veteran of Spitalfields and Portobello markets. Street chic and divine femininity sums up the look, and the collections are innovative, individual and impervious to trend-dependent purchasing. "My garments are edgy and eclectic but then again quite feminine," says Somi. "Arrogant Cat is about making it your own, wearing it your own way. It's not to impress other people, it's to express who you are and say this is my style." The list of celebrity converts includes Naomi Campbell, Natasha Bedingfield, Danii Minogue and Jodi Kidd.

■ **Bardot SC**
Cavern Walks,
Mathew Street L2 6RE
Tel: (0151) 258 1100
Newly-opened stockists of designer lingerie from Cotton Club, Muse, Tabooboo, La Perla, Mikey, Atuzo, and gorgeous premises on the second floor of Cavern designer Shopping Centre.

Location key:

PH Pier Head/Albert Dock
BD Business District
SC Shopping Centre
CQ Cultural Quarter
RW Rope Walks
HQ Hope Quarter

What did we tell you about feet on seats?

Caroline Oates RW
16-18 Newington Street L1 3RG
Tel: **(0151) 709 8359**
Discerning Liverpool and Ibiza clubbers descend upon her funky little emporium off Bold Street, where the lady herself designs and manufactures her own affordable garments.

Cricket SC
Cavern Walks,
Mathew Street L2 6RE
Tel: **(0151) 207 4645**
Everyone who's anyone shops here. A beautifully laid-out boutique with its very own upstairs catwalk, it stocks all those Stella, Roland Mouret, Pucci and Missoni must-haves you've been promising yourself, plus new treats from Lanvin, Stussy and Saff & Bide.

Designer City BD
14-16 Victoria Street L2 6QE
Tel: **(0151) 236 9115**
Five years old and going strong for this celebrated designer-label shop that now has its first women's collection featuring Sportmax, Sonia Rykiel, Amanda Wakeley, Prada Sport, Missoni Sport, Versace Sport, Armani Jeans...

Drome for Men SC
46 Bold Street L1 4DS
Tel: **(0151) 709 1441**
Cutting-edge and imaginative menswear and accessories from the only Liverpool store mentioned in Caryn Franklin's respected Fashion UK directory. Cutting-edge labels like Holland Esq., Edwin Jeans (direct from Japan), and G-Star, plus vintage Ralph Lauren and Burro.

Drome Couture/Women SC
Cavern Walks L2 6RE
Tel: **(0151) 255 0525/1565**
Couture (the upstairs bit in Cavern Walks) was recently reviewed by the Sunday Times as 'styled like a New York gallery' and includes Dolce & Gabbana, Cavalli, Gharani Strok, Betsey Johnson and Pringle Gold Label among its many cutting-edge collections. Women (downstairs) has funky stuff from Michiko Koshino, Guess, Miss Sixty, Diesel, Paul Frank and Stussy. Lots of awards, no surprises.

Giancarlo Ricci SC
45 Bold Street L1 4AL
Tel: **(0151) 708 8044**
Male and female fashion, from Armani to Versace, in this popular gentlemen's boutique situated near to Karen Millen.

3 Beat, Slater Street. At the forefront of worldwide house music for 10 years and now showcasing fresh new label talent. An honorable mention for nearby Bold Street Records, too.

Probe, Wood Street. Original and still the best, glam queen Pete Burns' old vinyl emporium is now opposite the old Liverpool Palace site.

Phase Records, Gostins Arcade, Hanover Street. House, funky house, Scouse house, drum 'n' bass and breakbeat.

■ **Jeff's SC**
80 Bold Street L1 4HR
Tel: **(0151) 707 0880**
Visit: **jeffsofboldst.co.uk**
One of the city's leading independent stores and affectionately known as the Harrods of Liverpool. Three floors of ladies fashion, a personal-dresser service, Victorian tea-room and 250-year-old wishing well.

■ **Lacoste SC**
18 Whitechapel L1 6DS
Tel: **(0151) 227 2214**
Actually Wade Smith's Lacoste Boutique. The French label decamped here in 2004 with a curved-white-wall concept for its store interior, the result of a collaboration between Paris-based architect Patrick Rubin and interior designer Christophe Pillet. It's their largest store in the UK.

■ **Loki SC**
Cavern Walks L2 6SE
Tel: **(0151) 255 1881**
Corset tops to die for, or at least gasp. Loki's designs have been used by national newspapers and described as 'garments for women who ooze femininity'.

■ **Microzine RW**
65-67 Bold Street L1 4EZ
Visit: **microzine.co.uk**
Men's 'concept' store selling everything from sports cars to fruit and vegetables to fashion. The idea is one of ever-evolving stock with fashion, furnishing, art, gadgets and technology. Also available: limited-edition, vintage and exclusive stock that appeals to the keener male shopper.

■ **Open SC**
54 Church Street L1 3AY
Tel: **(0151) 708 3322**
Through the arched entrance and into a cornucopia of designer clothing and concessions. How about that limited-edition Che Guevara replica jacket as worn by Cameron Diaz?

■ **Paloma SC**
2 Cavern Walks L2 6RE
Tel: **(0151) 236 6373**
Liverpool's own designer footwear shop – and the only one in the country to feature exclusive collections from Le Silla, Giuseppe Zanotti, Alexander McQueen, John Galliano and Pura Lopez.

■ **Peach Designer Wear SC**
22 Sir Thomas Street L1 6BW
Tel: **(0151) 255 1121**
Visit: **peachdesignerwear.co.uk**
Exclusive fashion from the world's top designers, among them Primp tracksuits, Esther Franklin's floaty fabrics, Love Kylie lingerie and Rock & Republic's edgy denim.

■ **Pure Woman SC**
6 Cavern Walks L2 6RE
Tel: **(0151) 227 3795**
Over 30 exclusive designer labels including Italy's very exclusive Occhipinti collection of hand-made leather shoes.

■ **Reiss SC**
46-48 Stanley Street L1 6AL
Tel: **(0151) 227 9157**
Visit: **reiss.co.uk**
Just over the road from Wade Smith, award-winning, tailor-made clothes for style-conscious men and women.

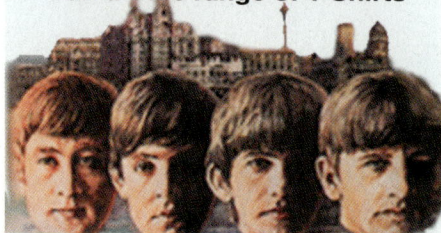

Script **HQ**
75-77 Lime Street L1 1JQ
Tel: **(0151) 709 1900**
Glad rags for male gadabouts.
Prada's the big seller, also Boss,
Armani, Dolce & Gabbana, Versace.

Sidewalk **RW**
**Petticoat Lane Arcade, 102 Bold
Street L1 4HY**
Tel: **(0151) 708 9697**
Menswear store stocking Armani,
Prada, Versace, Lacoste and Boss.

Vivienne Westwood **SC**
8 Mathew Street L2 6RE
Tel: **0151) 227 2700**
Visit: **hervia.com**
Wonderful clothes, and also
lots of fabulous accessories.
"My clothes are not about being
a consumer, they're about being
an individual," says the lady
herself. She's the first international
designer to open a stand-alone
store in the city, with all of her lines
– for men and women – housed
in the Cavern Walks boutique.
That means Gold Label, Red Label,
Man and Anglomania, plus shoes,
bags, sunglasses, jewellery,
perfume and eyewear. And who
else but shock rocker Marilyn
Manson – and wife Dita – to model
her latest spectacular collections?

Wade Smith **SC**
Mathew Street L2 6RE
Tel: **(0151) 255 1077**
Ultra-successful store synonymous
with the city's style. Four floors of
high fashion frequented by famous
names, it was founded by David
Wade-Smith, now director of the
funky Room Store on Albert Dock.
Latest collections include Huge.n
by local footballer Eugene Dadi.

Lady in red, ferry nice. Dress from Coast
on Rainford Square (off Mathew Street)

All dressed up

Why Liverpool starts the trends and never follows the herd...

Arrogant Cat.
Just purr-fect

■ Around autumn 2002, mumurings of 'Livercool' began appearing in the news. Kira Joliffe, editor of style mag Cheapdate, said Scousers had "a great sense of fashion, they make so much effort and look so perfect." The superlatives gathered pace six months later when Isabella Blow, champion of new talent and fashion director of Tatler, ran a photo-shoot in the city and declared it "a place where tradition meets cutting-edge."

Liverpudlians always have had their own cute sense of style. Trendsetters rather than followers, they don't heed national notions of what's in or out, new or old, but do their own thing with a swagger. They were among the first in the UK to wear denim, brought in by sailors from America after the Second World War, and the Merseybeat scene had its own code of sharp dress. When the rest of the country embraced punk, Liverpool's youth went electronic and adopted a softer look.

This was the era of a club called Eric's. Pete Burns was flogging Westwood out of the back of Probe, Julian Cope was starting a flying-jacket trend all by himself, and in 1984 Frankie Goes To Hollywood launched the must-have garment of the year with a take on Katharine Hamnett's famous 'Ban Nuclear Weapons Now' T-shirt. Every wannabe fashionista wore one bearing the legend 'Frankie Says Relax Don't Do It'.

Liverpudlians also invented terrace fashion. 'Scallies' appeared in the late 70s (the south responded with 'casuals'), Liverpool FC fans with wedge haircuts and foreign sports labels acquired while watching their team in Europe. When the look caught on, they moved on. They wore semi-flares in the mid-80s and by the time it took hold nationwide they'd adopted the 'country gent' look of Barbours and tweed. Tracksuits came next and have remained an idiosyncrasy of Scouse street style ever since. Worn with the bottoms tucked into socks, and always Lacoste.

Worth the journey...

Head up to Crosby for Encore, the fashion boutique nominated for the highly coveted Young Independent Fashion Retailer Of The Year award, organised by Drapers Record magazine (the fash bizz bible). Is Encore hip? Ask Paul Smith. He's allowed his Collection 2005 to be exclusively stocked there. Nearby is Sub Urban, offering new and unique garments like local pop artist Dave White's world-renowned, screen-printed sneaker T-shirts – the only place to find them outside London. And check out Knowsley-based Nook and Willow's website (nookandwillow.com) for unique, tailormade and absolutely fabulous accessories that have that 'somewhere to go' look for women.

There's no one Liverpool look, but there is a collective desire to dress up – from the teengirl sub-culture of pyjamas to full-on glamour in the city's bars personified on Grand National Ladies Day when the best-dressed punter drives home in a new Jag.

Contrast is key and it shows in the plethora of shops. Wade Smith is the original designer boutique and forerunner to Cricket and Drome. Now comes Vivienne Westwood, whose canon 'Dress up more than down because then you'll have a great time' could've been written for the city. Store manager Jonathan Weir adds, "Liverpool is a good-looking city and this is mirrored by the people who love to dress up and dress well. The women are adventurous and have their own direction. And that sums up Westwood."

Vintage may be a byword now, but it's had a following in Liverpool for decades. 69A (Renshaw Street) has been established for 20 years, while Bulletproof (Hardman Street) sells its 60s and 70s clothes by weight. With retro concessions, a flea market and local designers, Quiggins on School Lane has been a Liverpool institution. Over on Hanover Street is the Gostins Arcade, housing independent outlets selling retro clothes and urbanwear.

Liverpudlians aren't just wearing it, they're designing it. Paula McCullock, under her label Prudence Wildeblood, showed her collection at London Fashion Week. Jason Ansell saw his first collection snapped up by Wade Smith. The Felix Blow Partnership has built up a loyal following for its 8703 brand. And an exhibition by JMU's fashion students, won rave reviews – a sure sign the future is bright.

That's never been in doubt. After his magazine's photoshoot, Tatler editor Geordie Greig stated, "This is a super-sexy place, soon the whole world will catch on that Liverpool is having another renaissance." True, maybe, for fashion followers. But for Liverpudlians it's definitely a case of business as usual.

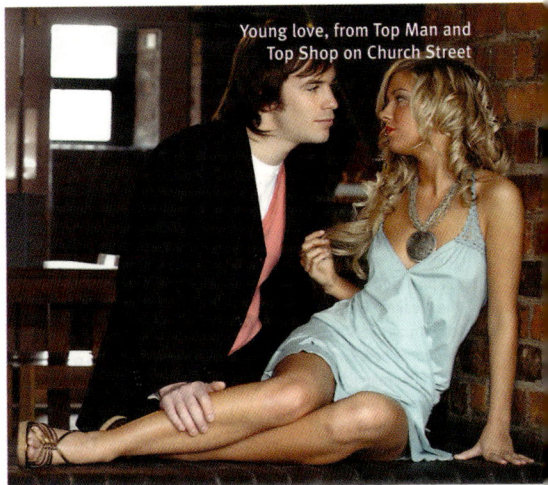

Young love, from Top Man and Top Shop on Church Street

Huge.n by Eugene Dadi (right), now at Wade Smith

Cu...

He...
wil...
a r...
Str...
a h...
out...
nev...
sal...
is s...
bel...
bec...
– T...
And...
exp...
of t...
figu...
tod...
Hai...
and...
nan...
is c...
lux...
offe...
col...
dre...
spe...
whi...
Bea...
foc...
trea...
mar...
wax...
faci...
call...

Introducing...

World Museum

Think you know Liverpool's wealth of wonderful museums and galleries? Think again. New for 2005 is the state-of-the-art World Museum on William Brown Street. Walk through the the stunning new entrance – underneath the giant flying Pterosaur – and head for the World Cultures gallery and its fascinating insights into the planet's rich and diverse cultures. On to a fabulous underwater world at the Aquarium, then creepie-crawlies galore at the Bug House – not least the giant wriggling spider and fly waiting as you walk in! Catch your breath at the Treasure House Theatre where World Museum's magnificent collections are brought to life through live performances and talks, and check out the Clore Natural History Centre (twice as big as the old attraction) and Weston Discovery Centre, a new hands-on attraction featuring 700 objects from the Museum's collections. And don't forget the brand new shop, with a full range of fair-trade stock and fab gifts. Visit: **worldmuseumliverpool.org.uk**

Where the art is

Presenting a munificence of museums and galleries...

In December 2003, Sir Jeremy Isaacs gave a speech at FACT. The former director general of the Royal Opera House was also chairman of the judging panel that, six months earlier, had chosen Liverpool as European Capital of Culture for 2008. "Without question," he told a full house, "this city has the greatest single conglomeration of galleries and museums of any city outside London – and that is a very strong calling card indeed." Shall we see what he means?

National Museums Liverpool

He's Henry VIII, he is

■ **National Museums Liverpool**
Tel: (0151) 207 0001
Visit: liverpoolmuseums.org.uk
This is the collective name for the eight museums and galleries that make up the greatest collection of artefacts, paintings and specimens collectively held under single ownership in the country. They are: the Conservation Centre, Lady Lever Art Gallery, Liverpool Museum, Merseyside Maritime Museum and HM Customs & Excise National Museum, Museum of Liverpool Life, Sudley House and the Walker Art Gallery.

For two years running, over 1.5million visitors have flocked to them. In 2004, NML was awarded the Freedom of Liverpool, and in 2008 all of its venues will be open for 24 hours to celebrate Die Lange Nacht on midsummer's night, the longest night of the year. As it is, they're open Monday to Saturday 10am-5pm, Sunday 12-5pm unless stated, and entrance to all exhibitions and events is free.

■ **Conservation Centre SC**
Whitechapel L1 6HZ
Tel: (0151) 478 4999
Visit: conservationcentre.org.uk
Awards galore for the UK's first national conservation centre, housed in a Victorian goods office. It leads the way in laser-cleaning (to remove surface layers of dirt of statues) and 3D digital scanning (to produce highly accurate replicas replacing original works threatened with further damage). The female personification of Liverpool, once on the roof of the Walker and now in the Centre's foyer, is the perfect example.

Location key:

PH Pier Head/Albert Dock
BD Business District
SC Shopping Centre
CQ Cultural Quarter
RW Rope Walks
HQ Hope Quarter

Lady Lever Art Gallery
Port Sunlight Village CH62 5EQ
Tel: **(0151) 478 4136**
Over the water for the collected
art treasures of Edwardian
philanthropist and soap magnate,
William Hesketh Lever. Summer
2005 brought Beside the Seaside,
an exhibition of late 19th Century
paintings celebrating fun by the
sea and including work by Walter
Sickert. The gallery also has
memorabilia relating to Lever's
fascination with Napoleon.

World Museum Liverpool **CQ**
William Brown Street L3 8EN
Tel: **(0151) 478 4399**
One of the country's premier
museums, now boasting a stunning
extension with a six-storey, glass-
topped atrium. Flying dinosaurs,
giant bugs, an aquarium and
fascinating World Cultures gallery.
African tribal masks, Eskimo hats,
Tibetan guardian lions, ancient
Egyptian tombstones, Japanese
shogun armour and Native
American head dresses. If it's out
there, it's in here.

Merseyside Maritime Museum and HM Customs and Excise National Museum **PH**
Albert Dock L3 4AQ
Tel: **(0151) 478 4499**
Tells the story of one of the world's
greatest ports and the people who
used it. Find out what it felt like to
cross mighty oceans as an emigrant
or a slave. Experience the palatial
world of liners like the Titanic and
Lusitania. And explore the history
of smuggling since the 1700s. Four
floors of exhibitions reflecting
Liverpool's seafaring heritage.

Water babies at Lady Lever

Pterosaurs at World Museum

Liners off Liverpool, in the Maritime Museum

Pre-Raphaelites at Sudley House

Museum of Liverpool Life PH
Pier Head L3 1PZ
Tel: **(0151) 478 4080**
From a statue of Billy Fury, the country's first great rock 'n' roller, to authentic pieces of the old Spion Kop, this is the ultimate celebration of Liverpudlian culture.

Most recently it's celebrated the city's diverse religious traditions, life on the Mersey in Roman times, the legendary Eric's club of the late 70s and early 80s, and the tragic original Beatle, Stuart Sutcliffe.

Sudley House
Mossley Hill Road, L18 8BX
Tel: **(0151) 724 3245**
You'll have to hang on until April 2006 before this former home of a wealthy Victorian ship-owner re-opens to the public, by which time a refurbishment will show masterpieces by Gainsborough, Turner, and the Pre-Raphaelites in all their glory.

The Walker CQ
William Brown Street L3 8EL
Tel: **(0151) 478 4199**
The first British public art gallery and one of the finest in Europe. The full-length Henry VIII portrait is thought to have belonged his favourite wife Jane Seymour, while William Hogarth's 1745 painting of David Garrick as Richard III captures the Marlon Brando of his day in full method-acting mode.

John Brett's The Stonebreaker is the favourite painting of Sir Peter Blake (designer behind the Beatles Sgt Pepper album cover), who calls it "a tiny, jewel-like painting among a superb collection." And the Tinted Venus, whose flesh-coloured body, blue eyes and golden hair caused a scandal when she was shown in London in 1862, is the beloved creation of local neo-classical sculptor John Gibson. He was loathe to give her up, writing to the wife of the rich Liverpool patron who commissioned him: "It would be as difficult for me to part with her as it would be for your husband to part with you."

Have we mentioned the Rubens, Rembrandt, Seurat, Cezanne, Poussin, Degas, Freud, Hockney, Gilbert and George?

David bow-wow-Bowie (ahem) at the Walker

Take your pic...

■ This startling image of David Bowie with scary hound is from Terry O'Neill: Celebrity, a photo exhibition running at the Walker Gallery till September 2005 and featuring 43 portraits of the most famous faces from the last four decades (the Beatles, Rolling Stones, Twiggy, Bridget Bardot, Woody Allen and Mia Farrow, Paul Newman and Lee Marvin, Ringo Starr and Barbara Bach etc). Late in 2004, the Conservation Centre had Britain's 50 Best Dressed Men, a fab collection chosen by Getty Images and GQ magazine that celebrated charisma and style and featured the likes of Cary Grant, Robbie Williams, John Gielgud, Roger Moore, Michael Caine, Peter Sellers, Winston Churchill and even Johnny Rotten.

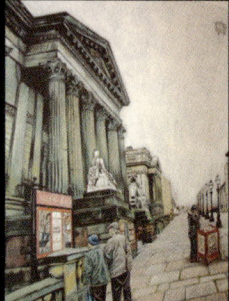

Museums and galleries

Bluecoat Arts Centre/ Display Centre SC

School Lane L1 3BX
Tel: **(0151) 709 5297**
Visit: **bluecoatartscentre.com /
bluecoatdisplaycentre.com**

The Grade I listed cornerstone of Liverpool's artistic life, and currently undergoing an exciting refurbishment of its studios, stages, workshops and galleries (the Display Centre is still open). With a continuous programme of innovative exhibitions and events, BAC has pioneered the visual and performing arts for decades.

In 2004 BDC was one of only six British galleries outside London represented at COLLECT at the V&A – the UK's first annual fair exclusively for contemporary applied decorative art.

Central Library and Record Office CQ

William Brown Street L3 8EW
Tel: **(0151) 233 5835**

Its Picton Reading Room is a work of art in itself. Don't miss John James Audubon's magnificent Birds of America book and the equally rare volumes in the Hornby Library and Oak Room.

CUBE RW

82 Wood Street L1 4DQ
Visit: **cube.org.uk**

As in, Centre for the Understanding of the Built Environment. Near the Tea Factory in the raucous lower reaches of Rope Walks, in 2004 it secured the first UK exhibition of David Adjaye, who designed the Nobel Peace Centre in Oslo and the award-winning Social night club in London's West End.

Decorative arts at Bluecoat Display Centre

World Discovery Centre aka Central Library

Red rooms at CUBE

Best of 3...
Beatles art

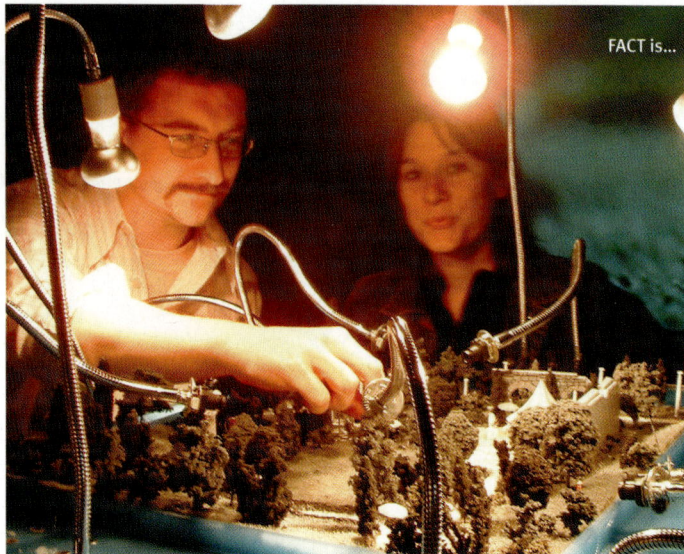

■ **View II Gallery,** Mathew Street. Unconventional art like Alex Corina's marvellous 'Mona Lennon' on tins cans, tiles and dustbin lids.

■ **Mathew Street Gallery.** Rare classics like Robert Whittaker's candid backstage shots in Munich and Abbey Road from the mid-60s.

■ **The Lobby,** Victoria Street. Artist Stephen Bowers' excellent neo-impressionist portraits of the Fabs in the early days.

■ **FACT RW**
88 Wood Street L1 4DQ
Tel: **(0151) 707 4450**
Visit: **fact.co.uk**
As in, Foundation for Arts and Creative Technology. Since it opened its sliding doors in 2003, half-a-million people have now visited Liverpool's 'arts project for the digital age' (the first new building dedicated to the arts since the Philharmonic Hall in 1939). Inside the £11million complex, you'll find two galleries dedicated to new media artwork, and three state-of-the-art cinemas showing arthouse and mainstream movies. There's a dinky clubhouse for hire called The Box, plus cafés and bars with great views across the Liverpool cityscape. It's an unparalleled support system for UK artists and another icon of Liverpool's cultural renaissance.

■ **Liverpool Academy of Arts RW**
36 Seel Street L45 7PA
Tel: **(0151) 709 0735**
Visit: **la-art.co.uk**
Dating back to 1763, the LAA is currently a small gallery dedicated to local artists, with an annual Beatles Art exhibition (last week in July to first in September).

■ **Open Eye Gallery RW**
28-32 Wood Street L1 4AQ
Tel: **(0151) 709 9460**
Visit: **openeye.org.uk**
Long-established, much-loved and showcasing innovative and challenging photography and media art with an international pedigree, including many world premieres and talks by the artists themselves. From abstract and detached images of the modern world to the power of the veil in Islamic society.

Tate Liverpool PH
Albert Dock L3 4BB
Tel: **(0151) 702 7400**
Visit: **tate.org.uk/liverpool**
Otherwise known as the National
Collection of Modern Art in the
North of England. Around 600,000
visitors a year admire its works
from the Tate Collection and special
exhibitions of contemporary art,
and past shows include Pablo
Picasso (featuring his Weeping
Woman of 1937), Salvador Dali
and Paul Nash. It's got a global
reputation, and you'd be mad to
miss it. Open Tuesday to Sunday
10am-5.50pm.

University of Liverpool
Art Gallery HQ
6 Abercromby Square L69 7WY
Tel: **(0151) 794 2348**
Visit: **liv.ac.uk/artgall**
Works by Turner, Epstein and
Freud, plus American wildlife artist
JJ Aubudon, all displayed in a
beautiful Georgian terrace house.

View Two Gallery SC
23 Mathew Street L2 6RE
Tel: **(0151) 236 9444**
Visit: **viewtwogallery.co.uk**
Three floors of wonderfully eclectic
work by local and global artists in
an informal venue on Liverpool's
Carnaby Street. There's a licensed
bar, too, though staff will be just
as happy to make you a cup of tea.

Western Approaches Museum BD
1-3 Rumford Street L2 3SZ
Tel: **(0151) 227 2008**
A permanent reminder of
Liverpool's role as Area Command
HQ for the Battle of the Atlantic.
Eerie, underground, awe-inspiring.

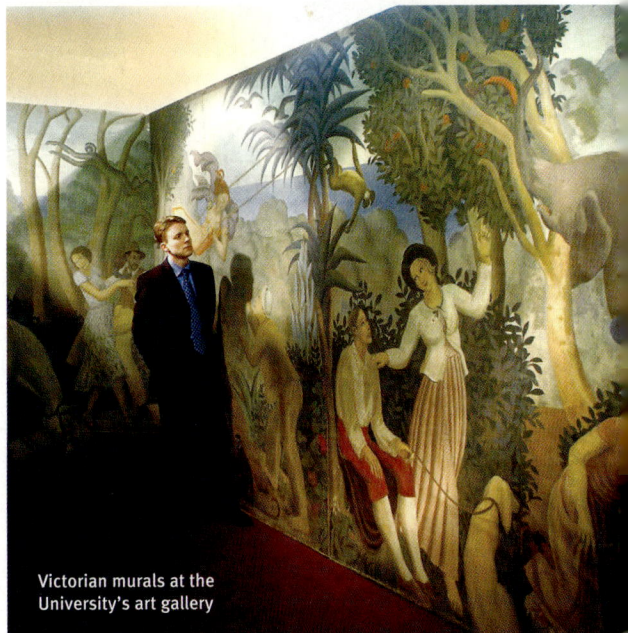

Victorian murals at the
University's art gallery

Art beat

■ "Birds are the angels of this earth and they represent freedom." With that rarefied explanation, conceptual artist Tracey Emin unveiled her gift to Liverpool ("one of my favourite cities") and her first piece of public art, early in 2005. Called Roman Standard and inspired by the Liver Bird, it takes the form of a bronze sparrow-like bird atop a four-metre high pole, and it's behind the Oratory gates next to the Anglican Cathedral. "It represents strength but also femininity," she adds. "Most public sculptures are a symbol of power which I find oppressive and dark. I wanted something that had a magic and an alchemy, something which would appear and disappear and not dominate."

Emin's public art follows other new arrivals in the city like Penelope, the twisting, glowing steel sculpture in Wolstenholme Square by Cuban artist Jorge Pardo (a reference to both Liverpool's maritime past and the unshakable faith of Ulysses' wife in the ancient Greek myth) and the Faces of Liverpool in blue glass portholes around Beetham Tower (celebrating the city's global connections and diverse culture with images of its contemporary residents).

Among the best post-war public sculptures are Patrick Glyn Heesom's 'growing thresh of wings' outside the Litttlewoods Building on Old Hall Street, the Piazza Waterfall at Beetham Plaza designed by Richard Huws to recreate the sound and fury of 'the restless, temperamental sea', and Charlotte Mayer's Sea Circle 'reflecting the constant coming

All because Tracy's tweet on Liverpool

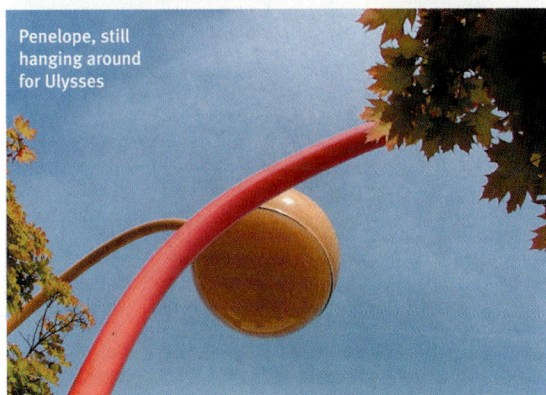

Penelope, still hanging around for Ulysses

Blue in the Face at Beetham Tower

Stained glass by Burne-Jones and Morris on Ullet Road

and going of men, women and ships to and from this great port'.

Other landmarks include The Great Escape, Edward Cronshaw's bronze sculpture of a man restraining a horse made of unravelling rope (top of Church Street), and A Case History, John King's stack of luggage piled on Hope Street's pavement for the city's first Biennial in 1998. The same year, SuperLambBanana (now relocated to Tithebarn Street from Wapping) was created by Japanese artist Taro Chiezo as a parody of genetic engineering. Seek out, too, older gems like the stained-glass window by Edward Burne-Jones and William Morris, in Ullet Road Unitarian Church just off Sefton Park in south Liverpool, and the Art Nouveau gates of the Philharmonic Hotel (Hope Quarter) that rival anything by Gaudi and the Modernists in Barcelona.

Excitingly, more and more art is appearing in Liverpool's bars, cafés and restaurants – and on the streets themselves. We urge you to view the murals of radical Liverpudlians by David Jacques in the Newz Bar (Water Street), Anthony Brown's portraits, abstracts and cityscapes in Colin's Bridewell, the Radisson SAS hotel and Hemingway's respectively, and the fabulous and often very famous works hanging in top restaurant 60 Hope Street. The 2006 Liverpool Biennial will once more appropriate the public landscape, and of late construction sites have been converted into outdoor galleries to both engage the public and chronicle the city's current eye-catching renaissance.

Sea Circle, top
of Copperas Hill

Introducing...

107.6 Juice FM

■ **107.6 Juice FM** knows how to party. For five years we've had a great line-up of shows, starting off the day with The Louis Hurst Breakfast Portion, through to Free Radio Juice where Liverpool gets to 'choose the choons', then onto specialist shows and more live OBs than you can shake a stick at! And the Juice listener certainly knows how to party! Living for the weekend is something other people do – and who can be bothered waiting until Friday?! Without a doubt Liverpool is the most happening city in the country. Everywhere you look there are new bars and clubs springing up – and the typical clubber, whether local or visiting, always makes the effort. Here at Juice, we're proud of the fact that our presenters come from Liverpool. In short, it means that they know what they're talking about. Plus, come the weekend Juice broadcasts over 10 hours of live music from four of the city's top clubs. So even if you're staying in, you can still be out! Juice FM. In Liverpool, it's where it's at.

Performance

From beautiful ballet to sleazy urban sounds...

■ The finest opera and classical evenings at the Empire and Phil. The best of modern drama and dance at the Everyman and Playhouse, Neptune and Unity, and LIPA. And a dozen top comedy and gig venues. Let us entertain you. We insist.

Location key:

PH Pier Head/Albert Dock
BD Business District
SC Shopping Centre
CQ Cultural Quarter
RW Rope Walks
HQ Hope Quarter

Clowning about
at the Empire

Classical and musicals

■ **Liverpool Empire Theatre CQ**
Lime Street L1 1JE
Tel: (0151) 708 3200
Visit: liverpoolempire.co.uk
The largest two-tiered theatre
in the country is also a visual treat,
all velvet seats, gilded décor,
brocaded curtains and dizzyingly
high ceiling. Only the Albert Hall
can hold a candle to this stunning
venue, recently refurbished and
now just as grand with state-of-
the-art facilities. Its 2005
programme included Cameron
Mackintosh's Miss Saigon (starring
Jon Jon Briones and Jennifer Hubilla
direct from the smash hit US tour),
The King and I, Tchaikovsky's
Sleeping Beauty and Swan Lake,
as well as regular and ever-popular
visitors Welsh National Opera and
Chinese State Circus. Whatever the
show, at night there's a sensational
view from the lounge bar across to
St George's Hall and William Brown
Street. Sublime.

■ **Liverpool Institute
of Performing Arts HQ**
Mount Street L1 9HF
Tel: (0151) 709 4988
Visit: lipa.ac.uk
Tomorrow's stars today. LIPA runs
two seasons of public productions
(dance, drama and musicals) each
year with students performing in up
to 30 shows in the Paul McCartney
Auditorium and Sennheiser Studio
Theatre – watch out for their
evenings of show-stopping jazz.
The 2005 season included Stephen
Sondheim's Into The Woods, a
collaboration with Music Theatre
International of New York, and Judy
Garland, a musical written and
performed by a final-year student.

■ **Philharmonic Hall HQ**
Hope Street L1 9BP
Tel: (0151) 709 3789
Visit: liverpoolphil.com
Home to the Royal Liverpool
Philharmonic Orchestra – and so
much more. There's a youth
orchestra and gospel choir, and the
hall regularly hosts gigs and world
music concerts (from Bacharach to
Buena Vista) plus audiences with
intellectuals and raconteurs. Once
you've admired the décor's riot of
musical motifs, close your eyes and
let some of the world's best
musicians serenade you. Have we
mentioned the movies yet? Classic
Films at the Phil features everything
from the Parisian splendour of
Moulin Rouge to the hard-boiled
noir of the Coen brothers, shown
on the world's only surviving
Walturdaw cinema screen. What's
one of those? A screen with a
proscenium that's raised through
the stage via a system of antique
counterweights. That's what.

New production of
The Odyssey, again
at the Empire

Drama and dance

■ **Everyman Theatre HQ**
Hope Street L1 9BH
Tel: (0151) 708 4776
Visit: everymanplayhouse.com
Live theatre in Liverpool is back and buzzing, with the Everyman and Playhouse under the dynamic leadership of directors Gemma Bodinetz and Deborah Aydon. The Everyman has a world-renowned reputation for staging ground-breaking work from the most talented directors, writers and actors in the business. In 2004 it staged classics like The Merchant of Venice and new work like Dael Orlandersmith's Yellowman, one of the most acclaimed plays in the US. And in 2005 it had a star-studded 40th birthday gala evening and launched a new programme of Made in Liverpool productions complemented by some of the best touring work around. It's simple: when you're in Liverpool, you've got to go to the Everyman.

■ **Neptune Theatre SC**
Hanover Street L1 3DY
Tel: (0151) 709 7844
Visit: neptunetheatre.co.uk
An intimate venue whose shows vary from classic drama to dance to children's plays. In 2005 it staged Hobson's Choice, one of the UK's best-loved comedy dramas, and there are regular clairvoyant and murder-mystery nights.

■ **The Playhouse SC**
Williamson Square L1 1EL
Tel: (0151) 709 4776
Visit: everymanplayhouse.com
Specialising in bold and creative interpretations of the very best drama. In 2005 it's put on Who's Afraid of Virginia Woolf? plus The Winter's Tale and Jamaica Inn, among many fine productions. This is, by the way, the oldest established repertory company in the country. So there.

■ **Unity Theatre HQ**
1 Hope Place L1 9BG
Tel: (0151) 709 4988
Visit: unitytheatreliverpool.co.uk
On the site of a synagogue and one of a select group of venues in the country formed before World War II 'to make theatres accessible to the great mass of the people'. It's maintained its reputation for staging innovative, adventurous work and regularly showcases rising talent from LIPA. There's children's theatre, too, plus a commitment to major city events (Writing on the Wall, Liverpool Comedy Festival and the Liverpool International Street Festival). Its patrons include actors Cathy Tyson, Ian Hart and Alison Steadman.

Making a song and dance about it

Everyman and Playhouse
put their cards on the table

LIVERPOOL PLAYHOUSE BUILT IN 1866,
HOUSED ENGLAND'S OLDEST REPERTORY
COMPANY AND WAS RESPONSIBLE FOR LAUNCHING
THE CAREERS OF SOME OF BRITAIN'S FINEST
ACTORS AND WRITERS.

THE EVERYMAN FOUNDED IN 1964,
QUICKLY BECAME A POWERFUL CREATIVE FORCE
WITH A SIMILAR RECORD FOR NURTURING LIVERPOOL'S
ACTING AND WRITING TALENT. FOLLOWING A DIFFICULT
PERIOD FOR BOTH THEATRES, THEY WERE MERGED
INTO A SINGLE ORGANISATION IN 1999.

LIVERPOOL EVERYMAN AND PLAYHOUSE
ARE CURRENTLY ENJOYING A CREATIVE REBIRTH.
THE THEATRES HAVE RETURNED TO FULL-TIME
PRODUCING, AND **MADE IN LIVERPOOL** NOW BEING
RECOGNISED AS A STAMP OF THEATRICAL QUALITY.

WITH THIS MAJOR EXPANSION IN PRODUCTION,
A PASSIONATE COMMITMENT TO NEW WRITING,
AND A RAPIDLY GROWING COMMUNITY
PROGRAMME; WE ARE ON AN EXCITING JOURNEY
TOWARDS LIVERPOOL'S YEAR AS EUROPEAN CAPITAL
OF CULTURE IN 2008. OUR MISSION IS FOR THESE
THEATRES TO BE FIRMLY ROOTED IN THEIR
COMMUNITY, YET BOTH NATIONAL AND
INTERNATIONAL IN SCOPE AND AMBITION.

FOR FURTHER INFORMATION ON LIVERPOOL EVERYMAN AND PLAYHOUSE
PLEASE CALL 0151 709 4776 OR SEE WWW.EVERYMANPLAYHOUSE.COM

EVERYMAN 13 HOPE STREET LIVERPOOL L1 9BH
PLAYHOUSE WILLIAMSON SQUARE LIVERPOOL L1 1EL

Comedy

Best of 3...
Scouse stand-ups

■ **Chris Cairns**. Razor-sharp wit hailing from the one and only Liverpool 8, and the city's 2003 Comedian of the Year.

■ **Keith Carter.** Man of many, many talents. Observe closely when he metamorphoses into cosmic uber-scally Nige, then try really hard not to laugh.

■ **Nathan McCullen.** Just 15 when he won Best New Comedian at the Liverpool Echo awards in 2003. How good's he gonna be when he grows up?

■ **The Laughterhouse BD**
13-15 Fenwick Street L2 7LS
Tel: (0151) 231 6881
Visit: laughterhouse.com
Established for three years now as a centre of comedic excellence, it's downstairs in the haunted (no kidding) cellar of the old alehouse. Four headline acts on a Saturday night and food (go for the red hot chilli platters) included in the price. Howard Marks has done a turn here, and Mark Thomas has topped the bill in the past.

■ **The Pilgrim HQ**
34 Pilgrim Street L1 9HB
Tel: (0151) 709 2302
Beatle-tastic basement pub near to LIPA and the Anglican Cathedral. It's got a hugely popular Dead Good Poets Society and a new monthly comedy night upstairs that's starting to take off, run by drama students from John Moores University. Dig the Rubber Soul art.

■ **Rawhide @ Central Hall HQ**
Roscoe Gardens
Mount Pleasant L3 5SA
Tel: (0151) 726 2400
Visit: rawhidecomedy.com
Just recently relocated from the cool Blue Bar & Grill on the Albert Dock to classical Central Hall on Renshaw Street, this is the city's original stand-up show. In 2004 it hosted the Liverpool leg of Channel 4's So You Think You're Funny? And the roll-call of usual suspects reads like this: Steve Gribbin, Reginald D Hunter, Ian Cognito, Brendan Dempsey, Junior Simpson, Mitch Benn, Steve Best, Phil Nichol, Simon Evans, Marty Wilson, Colin Cole, Tony Burgess, Martin Beaumont and, of course, Keith Carter as lovable Liverpool scally Nige. We'd also like to draw your attention to Rawhide's Singing Hamsters. They sing the Rawhide theme, cost £7.50 and are 'supremely entertaining when drunk'. By all accounts.

Applause in the proceedings

All that jazz

■ An annual Liverpool jazz festival is on the way. As it is, Victoria Street is already becoming something of a jazz quarter, with live music at Pizza Express, the Place and Metro Eating Room & Bar, while the likes of Heart and Soul (Mount Pleasant), Blundell Street and the Residents Bar at Hope Street Hotel regularly showcase both solo performers and groups. Liverpool Jazz is an umbrella organisation that encourages live sessions at venues as diverse as LIPA and Sefton Park's Palm House, while the Southport Jazz festival goes from strength to strength, with artists such as the legendary Georgie Fame, precocious Kyle Eastwood (son of Clint) and sensational Gwyneth Herbert appearing in 2005.

Gigs

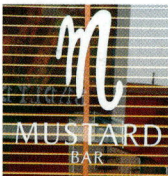

■ **Carling Academy CQ**
11-13 Hotham Street L3 5UF
Tel: (0151) 256 5555
Visit: liverpool-academy.co.uk
You're just around the corner from Lime Street and the Empire Theatre (on the site of the old Lomax) in a rocking joint opened autumn 2003. The main auditorium holds 1,200 and hosts legends and upstarts in equal measure. The 500-capacity Academy 2 showcases rising talent, while Subculture is two rooms of rock and alternative music with guest deejays like the Von Bondies.

■ **Liverpool Academy HQ**
University of Liverpool
Guild of Students,
160 Mount Pleasant L69 7BR
Tel: (0151) 794 6868
Academy 1 is the biggie (2,000-capacity) that's been graced by the Thrills, Coldplay, Elvis Costello, Mercury Rev etc. Academy 2 holds 400 and has welcomed The Vines, The Fall, Lloyd Cole and Cooper

Temple Clause. Last up, Academy 3 with space for 150 and a stage for upcoming acts. The entire venue also hosts Double Vision, a massive student night, every Monday. Oh for Tuesday lie-ins...

■ **Royal Court CQ**
1 Roe Street L1 1HL
Tel: (0151) 709 4321
Visit: royalcourttheatre.net
Fully restored to its former Art Deco glory and hosting drama once again (past performers include John Gielgud, Margot Fonteyn and Richard Burton) as well as pop. The basement lounge is a replica of the one on the original Queen Mary.

■ **Zanzibar RW**
43 Seel Street L1 4AZ
Tel: (0151) 707 0633
The Coral came out of this place. Noel Gallagher's hung out here when recording at Parr Street. Great for rising local talent and catching the next big thing.

Jools Holland boogie-woogie s
on the banks of the Mersey

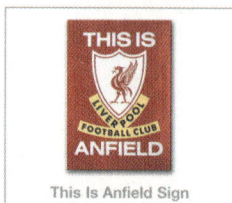

The thrills

Liverpool loves its sport. Do you prefer to watch or join in?

■ There's the Grand National, no other horse race quite like it. Two football clubs with the kind of pedigree others pine for. And so many great golf courses it's ever-so-slightly embarrassing. An international tennis tournament, too, plus excellent sailing facilities (of course) and some first-class gyms and luxury spa centres. In the zone yet?

Horse racing

■ **Aintree Racecourse**
Ormskirk Road, Aintree L9 5AS
Tel: **(0151) 523 2600**
Visit: **aintree.co.uk**
The John Smith's Grand National:
four miles and 856 yards that have
600million viewers glued to their
TV sets all over their globe. In
2005, Britons wagered a record
£200million on a single day's
sporting action as pre-race
favourite Hedgehunter, ridden
by Ruby Walsh, won the 158th
running. Aside from its blue riband
race Aintree pulls in 30,000
punters on an average racing day –

well ahead of Ascot and
Cheltenham – and £30million
has been set aside for two huge
grandstands and a brand new
parade ring for 2007.

■ **Haydock Park**
Newton-le-Willows WA12 0HQ
Tel: **01942 72596**
Visit: **haydock-park.com**
Over 250 years old and one of the
country's premier racecourses.
Every year there are 31 meetings
featuring both Flat and National
Hunt races and attracting 250,000
people. Off Junction 23 of the M6.

Football

■ **Everton FC**
Goodison Park L4 4EL
Tickets: **0870 442 1878**
Visit: **evertonfc.com**
If you know your history, this is
the first football club in England
to spend 100 years in the top flight
– a feat celebrated in 2003 – and
the one that's given the world two
magnificent centre-forwards from
different eras with the same world-
class credentials. Dixie Dean was
the first and only player to score
60 league goals in a season, back
in 1928. Former Blue Wayne
Rooney, now with Manchester
United, surely has a host of records
in front of him. After the glory years
of the mid-80s, the Blues are again
flying under current manager David
Moyes, who steered them into the
2005/06 UEFA Champions League,
and their supporters remain as
passionate and loyal as ever.
Get down to Goodison.

GRASS GROWS
BY THE INCH
RUINED
BY THE FOOT

Anfield Road L4 oTH
Ticket hotline: **0870 220 2345**
Visit: **liverpoolfc.tv**

There are the lucky, lucky ones who got to stand on the Spion Kop and sing Queen's We Are The Champions when it really was no1 in the charts and Liverpool had just clinched another title on some unremembered late spring evening. And there are the ones who have supported the team all their lives and not yet seen them play.

Either way, the feeling is the same when they've veered right from Scotland Road, up Everton Valley and onto Walton Breck Road, and got that first glimpse of the Kop Grandstand, its massive bulk dwarfing the adjacent terraced housing. Welcome to one of the most legendary sporting venues on the planet, the home of Liverpool Football Club and a shrine for hundreds of thousands of pilgrims worldwide. Arsenal, Chelsea and Manchester United may joust for the Premiership's top spot, but this club always stands alone.

Outside the superstore is a statue of Bill Shankly, mythical manager in the Swinging Sixties. Both 'the Shanks' and successor Bob Paisley – the only coach to guide a team to three European Cup victories – are commemorated by giant gates either side of the stadium, which also has a Hillsborough Memorial.

While new boss Rafa Benitez blends local talent with Spanish flair, the club's success on the pitch remains unsurpassed. Most recently six trophies have been won in the last five years, and the all-time haul of silverware is: four European Cups, three UEFA Cups, two European Super Cups, a record 18 League Championships, six FA Cups and seven League Cups. Many of the medals and plenty of memorabilia – from superstars like Kenny Dalglish and Steven Gerrard – are on show at the museum, where you'll also experience the electric atmosphere of the old Kop and the learn about the Liverpool anthem You'll Never Walk Alone.

A space-age 60,000-seater stadium is planned for the near future, so get up to the original Anfield while you still can.

Golf

**England's
Golf Coast...**

■ Merseyside has over 40 quality golf courses, including some of the UK's most challenging and beautiful venues, nestling between the pace of urban life and ruggedness of the coastline. Seven of them are leading Championship venues. As well Royal Liverpool and Royal Birkdale, there's Hillside in Southport and Formby Hall, host to the 2004 Curtis Cup. Now a new Festival of Golf is being staged at courses in Sefton and Wirral every year until at least 2006. Central to the week-long event will be the Merseyside English Seniors Open, forming part of the European Seniors Tour with household names like Sam Torrance, Tony Jacklin and Bernhard Gallacher. There's more at **englandsgolfcoast.com.**

■ **Royal Birkdale**
Waterloo Road, Southport PR8 2LX
Tel: **01704 567920**
Visit: **royalbirkdale.com**
Considered to be the best course in the country, Birkdale and its mighty sand dunes will stage the Open Championship for the ninth time in 2008. In the past it's seen greats like Arnold Palmer, Lee Trevino, Tom Watson and Mark O'Meara all lift the famous claret jug.

■ **Royal Liverpool**
Meols Drive, Hoylake CH47 4AL
Tel: **(0151) 632 3101**
Visit: **royal-liverpool-golf.com**
Another outstanding seaside links with a distinguished history (only Westward Ho! in Devon is older). It looks benign, plays tough and is likely to attract 250,000 people and 500million TV viewers for the British Open in 2006. It was on this quite corner of the Wirral in 1930 that Bobby Jones won the second leg of his famous Grand Slam.

Tennis

■ **Calderstones Park**
Childwall L18 3JD
Tel: **(0151) 227 5940**
Visit: **liverpooltennis.co.uk**
A gloriously green setting with 36 grass courts and a 5,000-seater stadium with a lakeside backdrop. In mid-June it hosts the Liverpool International Tennis Tournament, an eight-man, round-robin warm-up for Wimbledon with star names aplenty, and a Legends event that's featured the one and only Martina Navratilova, among others.

Cricket

■ **Liverpool Cricket Club**
**Aigburth Road,
Grassendale L19 3QF**
Tel: **(0151) 427 2930**
Visit: **liverpoolcricketclub.co.uk**
Stages Lancashire CC fixtures and was a firm favourite with Don Bradman. The pavilion has function rooms with views to the Welsh hills. As the playful website says, 'There is no finer way to spend a Saturday afternoon than watching a cricket match from the balcony with a pint of our finest beer at hand'...

Sailing and watersports

■ **Liverpool Yacht Club**
Coburg Wharf L3 4BP
Tel: **(0151) 281 8186**
Visit: **lyc.org.uk**
Located in the Marina &
Harbourside Club (340 permanent
pontoon berths), half-a-nautical-
mile from the scuba-diving centre
at Albert Dock, with races every
other weekend on the Mersey
and out to the Irish Sea. There
are also courses for newcomers
and regular day-trips and weekend
cruises along the beautiful coasts
of North and West Wales, the Isle
of Man, Cumbria and Scotland.
And you can hire the clubhouse
for anything from a buffet to
five-course meal.

Aviation

■ **Helicentre Liverpool**
John Lennon Airport L24 5GA
Tel: **(0151) 448 0388**
Visit: **helicentre.com**
Take a tour of Liverpool in a
helicopter, or a flying lesson as a
thrilling one-off experience or first
step to a Private Pilots Licence.

Climbing

■ **Awesome Walls Centre**
Athol Street L5 9XT
Tel: **(0151) 298 2422**
Visit: **awesomewalls.co.uk**
A mile from the city-centre, one
of the largest indoor climbing
centres in Europe with walls and
routes to suit all skill levels.

Fitness and well being

■ Absolution Gym
Britannia Pavilion,
Albert Dock L3 4AD
Tel: (0151) 707 9333
Gym, sauna, steam room,
professional beauty treatments
and spa with special one-day
guest packages.

■ Ark Health & Fitness
Radisson SAS Hotel,
107 Old Hall Street L3 9BD
Tel: (0151) 966 1500
Visit: radissonsas.com
Three-levels with pool, jacuzzi,
steam room, sauna, gym and
beauty treatments in one of
the city's newest and most
prestigious hotels.

■ Club Spa
Crowne Plaza Hotel,
St Nicholas Place L3 1QW
Tel: (0151) 243 8243
Visit: cpliverpool.com
Therapeutic massage that
enhances well-being and reduces
tension, plus aromatherapy
massage to treat a range of
physiological conditions.

■ David Lloyd
6 The Aerodrome, Speke L24 8QD
Tel: (0151) 494 4000
Visit: davidlloydleisure.co.uk
Arguably the most comprehensive
health, fitness and racquets
facility in Liverpool, located in a
remarkable building – a renovation
of one of the hangars on the old
airport site.

■ Greens Health & Fitness
1 Riverside Drive L3 4EN
Tel: (0151) 707 6000
Visit: greensonline.co.uk

Unisex beauty treatments, pool,
aroma steamroom, sun showers
and exercise rooms with women-
only classes, plus bar, brasserie
and take-home food service.

■ Leisure Club
Marriott City Centre Hotel,
Queen Square L1 1RH
Tel: (0151) 476 8000
Swimming pool, solarium, fitness
centre plus aromatherapy,
reflexology and massage.

Holistic

■ Alternative therapies
Astanga Vinyasa Yoga
13 Arrad Street L7 7BQ
Tel: (0151) 639 5776
Classical postures in a continuous
sequence. But bring your own mat!

■ The Health Place
Blackburne House,
Hope Street L8 7PE
Tel: (0151) 709 4356
Visit: blackburnehouse.co.uk
Holistic health and fitness for
women, with a range of therapies.

■ Massage & Flotation Centre
66A Lord Street L2 1TD
Tel: (0151) 709 9701
Visit: themassagecentre.co.uk
Specialising in flotation therapy,
plus massage treatments, body
wraps and special pamper days.

■ Chinese Acupuncture Centre
31 Rodney Street L1 9EH
Tel: (0151) 703 2938
Newly-opened, initial consultations
and 45-minute sessions.

Out of town

You are now 50 miles, as the Liver Bird flies, **from the highest peak in Wales (Snowdon)** and 65 miles from England's biggest mountain (Scafell Pike in the Lake District). **In-between, there's rather a lot going on...**

Greater Liverpool and Lancashire

■ South along Riverside Drive from the city-centre is the serene promenade at Otterspool (and giant beech trees in the adjacent park), and later Halewood Triangle Country Park (the region's oldest native woodland) plus the National Trust splendour of Speke Hall.

To the north-east there's Croxteth Hall & Country Park, an historic mansion in a wooded park, and Knowsley, home to the National Wildflower Centre and the Safari Park, the first of its kind to open by a large city and a haven for lions, tigers, elephants and rhino – and just recently the first-ever twin Pere David deer fawns to be successfully bred in captivity.

Due north from Waterloo is the Sefton Coast with its string of nature reserves. Formby Point is the fourth largest dune system in the country and home to one of Britain's last colonies of red squirrels and natterjack toads, as well as a wonderful array of birdlife such as oystercatchers, sanderlings, yellowhammers and greater spotted woodpeckers.

On to the elegant seaside resort of Southport, approximately 20 miles from Liverpool, with golden sands, green lawns, Victorian shopping arcades and a climate that boasts more sunshine hours than anywhere else in the North West of England.

Wirral and Cheshire

■ Directly opposite the Pier Head is Birkenhead, with its Norman Priory dating from 1150 and Historic Warships Centre at East Float Dock – check out the big, brooding U-Boat 534, the only German submarine raised from the seabed after being sunk by the Allies.

Nearby is the riverside development Twelve Quays from where two of Liverpool's three freight and passenger services to Ireland operate, and further north Seacombe's Aquarium (octopus, lobsters, crabs and a giant conger eel) and new £8million Astronomy & Space Centre, then New Brighton promenade and Fort Perch Rock.

Head south for Port Sunlight Heritage Centre (over 900 listed buildings and landscaped gardens) and Ellesmere Port's Boat Museum and Blue Planet Aquarium, featuring an underwater tunnel and huge window onto one the largest collections of sharks in the whole of Europe.

The other side of Wirral boasts West Kirby Marine Lake and promenade, and seal-spotting on the nearby Hilbre Islands Local Nature Reserve.

Due south is Wirral Country Park in Thurstaston (and its superb views across the Dee Estuary to Wales), the picturesque resort of Parkgate and Ness Botanic Gardens in Neston (owned by the University of Liverpool). From here you can see Moel Famau, the first big peak in North Wales, in its country park of gentle slopes and teeming wildlife. And you're a matter of minutes from the walled city of Chester, easily accessed on special trips by Merseyrail.

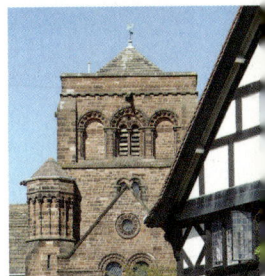

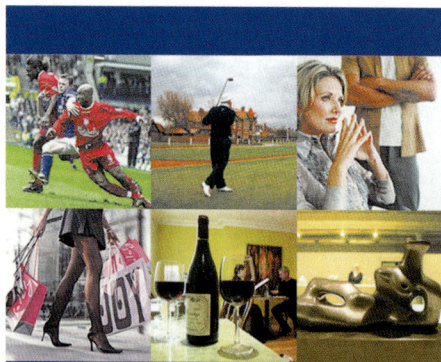

Details

Liverpool. The nitty gritty. If it's out there, it's in here.
Your handy directory of practical information...

Need more help? Look for Liverpool's information society...

■ The Big Screen has landed. Clayton Square's state-of-the-art addition (Shopping Centre) is operational 24 hours a day, broadcasting BBC shows as well as local info. The 08 Place (Whitechapel) is a new focal point for the Capital of Culture experience, providing tourist info, merchandise and a booking service, while the nearby Paradise Project's call-in centre on Lord Street has a huge scale model of the £800million site well worth a gander.

You'll also find a system of info panels all over the city-centre designed to make discovery easier. They feature a mapping system displaying iconic buildings in 3D and areas within six minutes walk – all in clear colours for visually-impaired people with clear identification of steps and areas inaccessible to wheelchair users.

On Church Street there's more help from a 'pavement pod' that opens up a whole new e-world for visitors and residents alike. Use it to find out about tourism, culture and sport, or to contact friends and relatives in the UK or overseas via free email, text messages and photomail (remember the phone area code for Liverpool is 0151; if you're calling overseas the prefix is +44). Information is available in English, Spanish, French, Chinese and Somali.

Outside FACT (Rope Walks) are five flashing beacons called metroscopes, the first UK sculptures to feed off information from the web, beaming live news from Liverpool's sister cities Shanghai, Cologne, Odessa and Dublin.

Tourist information
■ General enquiries
Tel: (0151) 709 5111/8111
or: 0906 680 6886
(calls cost 25p per minute)
■ Queen Square Centre
Mon-Sat 9am-5.30pm;
Sun & Bank Holidays.
10.30am-4.30pm
■ Albert Dock Centre
Atlantic Pavillion,
Albert Dock L3
Daily 10am-5.30pm.
■ Liverpool John Lennon Airport
Oct-Mar: daily 5am-11pm
Apr-Sept: daily 4am-12am

Accommodation service
■ Free accommodation booking
Tel: (0151) 709 8111
or: 0845 601 1125 (local call rate)
Visit: visitliverpool.com

Left luggage
■ Lime Street Station L1
Tel: (0151) 702 2219
Daily 7am-9pm (£4.50 per item).

Banks and exchange
■ Most of the city-centre's large hotels have bureau de change facilities for visitors. You can also change money at Liverpool's larger post offices. Basic opening hours Mon-Fri 9.30am-4.30pm.
■ Barclays
Whitechapel L1
Mon-Sat 9am-5pm.
■ American Express
54 Lord Street L2
(0151) 702 4501
Mon-Fri 9am-5.30pm; Sat 9am-5pm.
■ Thomas Cook
HSBC, 4 Dale Street L2
Commission free.

Post offices
■ Mon-Sat 9am-5.30pm
(unless stated).
■ Corn Exchange
India Building, Water Street L2
Mon-Fri 9am-5.30pm.
■ Exchange
82 Old Hall Street L3
Mon-Fri 8am-5.30pm.

■ Leece Street
35/37 Leece Street L1
Mon-Fri 8.45am-5.30pm;
Sat 8.45am-12.30pm.
■ Liverpool St Johns
St John's Centre, Houghton Way L1
Foreign currency exchange available.
■ Lyceum
1 Bold Street L1

Internet cafés
■ Café Latte.net
4 South Hunter Street L1
Tel: (0151) 708 9610
Mon-Fri 8am-9pm;
Sat-Sun 9am-5.30pm.
■ Planet Electra Internet Café
36 London Road L3
Tel: (0151) 280 7000
Mon-Fri 8am-9pm;
Sat-Sun 9am-5.30pm.

Shop opening times
Mon-Sat 9am-5.30pm;
Sun 11am-4.30pm
Small, independent shops
and markets may differ.

Getting here

■ Liverpool's location makes it easily accessible from all parts of the UK. There's a daily airlink between London and John Lennon Airport, which offers an increasing number of scheduled destinations (among them Rome, Milan, Venice, Budapest, Alicante, Amsterdam, Basel, Granada, Barcelona, Belfast, Berlin, Cologne, Dublin, Geneva, Gerona, Isle of Man, Madrid, Malaga, Nice, Palma, Paris, Limoges) and is well-connected to the city-centre. Regular ferry services run from Liverpool to Ireland, while Lime Street train station is a major rail terminus on the West Coast Line from London Euston and is also linked to Manchester Airport via the Merseyrail City Line. For cars and coaches, the motorway network is linked via the M62, M58, M57 and M3/M56.

■ **John Lennon Airport**
Tel: **(0151) 288 4000**
or: **0870 750 8484**
Visit: **liverpooljohnlennonairport.com**
In Speke, six miles to the south-east of the city-centre.

■ **VLM London-Liverpool**
Tel: **(0151) 236 9696**
or: **020 7476 6677**
Visit: **flyvlm.com**
Five flights every weekday between JLA and London City Airport in Docklands (three miles from Canary). A fast 15-min check-in and fares starting from £36.90 one-way.

■ **AirportXpress 500**
Tel: **(0151) 236 7676**
Buses from airport to city centre. From

5.15am-12.15am, 15 minutes past and 15 minutes to every hour (£2 adult, £1 child) seven days a week.

■ **National Rail Enquiries**
Tel: **0845 748 4950**
Visit: **thetrainline.co.uk**

■ **National Express Coaches**
Norton Street L3
Tel: **0870 580 8080**
Visit: **nationalexpress.com**
Operating regular services from all major towns and cities in the UK.

■ **Norse Merchant Ferries**
Tel: **(0151) 944 1010**
Regular service from Belfast and Dublin.

■ **P&O Irish Sea**
Tel: **0870 242 4777**
Visit: **poirishsea.com**
Early morning and overnight crossings from Dublin to Liverpool Freeport (Bootle) on the Norbank and Norbay ferries with two restaurant areas and lounges, a bar and en suite cabins.

■ **SeaCat/Isle of Man Steam Packet Co**
Tel: **0870 552 3523**
Visit: **steam-packet.com**
Room for 774 passengers and 175 cars onboard the SuperSeaCat from Dublin and the Isle of Man to Liverpool's Princes Dock Landing Stage (Pier Head). The engines, incidentally, were built by GEC Alstrom of Merseyside. Mar-Nov: daily service to Douglas IOM (2hrs 50mins) and Dublin (4hrs). Nov-Mar: weekend ferry to Douglas (4hrs).

Getting around

The River Mersey can be crossed by ferry, the two car tunnels and Merseyrail underground network, with regular trains between James Street and Hamilton Square. There's a comprehensive bus and train system, and a new tram scheme featuring a 10-stop city-centre loop will be fully operational by 2007.

■ **Traveline Merseyside**
Tel: **(0151) 236 7676**
(information on all local bus and train services)
or: **0870 608 2608** (public transport services throughout England, Scotland and Wales)

■ **Merseytravel**
Tel: **(0151) 236 7676**
Visit: **merseytravel.gov.uk**
Information, updates and tickets for public transport on buses, trains and ferries. Fares vary depending on journey and company used. Pay at point of departure or purchase Saveaway tickets from train stations, Merseytravel centres at Queen Square, Paradise Street and 24 Hatton Garden or from newsagents and post offices. Saveaway Tickets one-day passes for use on buses, trains and ferries from 9.30am-4pm and after 6pm, all day weekends and Bank Holidays. £2.10-£2.70 adult, £1.60-£1.90 under 15s.

■ **Merseyrail**
Tel: **(0151) 236 7676**
or: **0870 608 2608**
(calls charged at national rate)
Visit: **merseyrail.org**
Extensive urban rail network connecting the city of Liverpool with the rest of Merseyside: Southport, Ormskirk, Kirkby and Hunts Cross on the Northern Line; New Brighton, West Kirby, Chester and Ellesmere Port on the Wirral Line, including four city-centre underground stations (James Street, Moorfields, Lime Street and Central) and connections to other towns and cities.

Merseyrail NETWORK MAP

Northern Line — Wirral Line
City Line — Other Lines

Trio, Trioplus, Saveaway tickets and Free Travel Passes valid in this area

Trioplus tickets and Free Travel Passes valid on rail only in this area

Regular bus links run from Liverpool Central (Great Charlotte Street), James Street, Moorfields (Dale Street), Lime Street and Garston to Liverpool John Lennon Airport. Ring Traveline for details.

Frequent bus links between CHESTER STATION and CHESTER CITY CENTRE free to rail passengers.

Travel Information

traveline public transport info

0870 608 2 608 National Call Rate

OPEN 8AM TILL 8PM 7 DAYS A WEEK

www.merseytravel.gov.uk

Buses

Most major attractions can be reached by the city's SMART bus service, single-decker buses with facilities for wheelchairs and pushchairs. Main bus depots at Paradise Street and Queen Square.

Mersey Ferries

Tel: **(0151) 236 7676**
Visit: **merseyferries.co.uk**

Daily commuter service from Pier Head to Seacombe and Woodside on the Wirral. Mon-Fri 7.45-9.15am & 4.15-7.15pm, with hourly River Explorer Cruise service 10am-3pm; Sat-Sun 9.05-9.35am & 7pm, River Explorer Cruise 10am-6pm.

Taxis

The main black cab ranks are at Lime Street Station, James Street Station, Adelphi Hotel, Whitechapel, Sir Thomas Street, Great George Street and Chinatown.

Private hire taxis

Davy Liver Ltd
Tel: **(0151) 709 2031/4646**
Dial-A-Cab
Tel: **(0151) 480 8000**
Mersey Cabs
Tel: **(0151) 298 2222**

Car hire

National Car Rental
Tel: **(0151) 259 1316**
Visit: **nationalcar.com**
Skydrive UK Ltd
Tel: **(0151) 448 0000**
or: **07801 423500**

Absolute Class Chauffeur Services
Tel: **0800 587 4575**
Visit: **absoluteclass.uk.com**
Ansome Heritage Hire
(0151) 531 6947
Elite Chauffeur Services
Tel: **(0151) 292 8435**
Visit: **elitechauffeurs.co.uk**
First Company
Tel: **(0151) 236 5640**
Visit: **1stcompany.com**
INTX
Tel: **(0151) 727 7000**
Tel: **intxuk.com**

Coach hire

Matthews Travel
Tel: **(0151) 342 1833**
Visit: **coach2hire.com**
Maghull Coaches
Tel: **(0151) 933 2324**
Visit: **maghullcoaches.co.uk**
Maypole Coaches
Tel: **(0151) 547 2713**

NCP Car parks

John Lennon Airport L24
Tel: **(0151) 486 5689**
24-hour multi-storey.
Oldham Street L1
Tel: **(0151) 709 8727**
24-hour multi-storey.
Pall Mall L3
Tel: **(0151) 236 5738**
Mon-Fri 7.30am-7.30pm.
Newquay L1
Tel: **(0151) 227 1274**
Multi-storey Mon-Sat 7am-7pm.
Lime Street L3
Tel: **(0151) 709 7014**
24-hour multi-storey.
Moorfields L2
Tel: **(0151) 258 1390**
24-hour multi-storey.
Paradise Street L1
Tel: **(0151) 707 2455**
24-hour multi-storey.

Travellers with disabilities

Merseylink
Tel: **(0151) 709 1929**

Transport information service for people with disabilities.
Shopmobility
Tel: **(0151) 708 9993**
Dial UK
Tel: **01302 310 123**
Information and advice line.

Passports and visas

Liverpool Passport Office
101 Old Hall Street L3 9BD
Advice line: **0870 521 0410**
Visit: **passport.gov.uk**

UKPS provides a service at its public counters to customers who need a passport urgently, in less than two weeks. Appointment-only basis. Mon-Fri 8am-6pm; Sat 9am-3pm.

Emergency services

For the local police constabulary, fire service, ambulance or regional coastguard in an emergency, call 999 or 112. For a free home fire safety check, call the enquiry and appointment line 0800 731 5958.
Merseyside Police HQ
Canning Place
Tel: **(0151) 709 6010**
Visit: **merseyside.police.uk**
Merseyside Fire Service HQ
Bridle Road, Bootle
Tel: **(0151) 296 4000**
Visit: **merseyfire.gov.uk**
Transco Gas Emergency Service
Tel: **0800 111 999**
United Utilities (Water Leakline)
Tel: **0800 330 033**

Hospitals and medical

■ NHS Direct
Tel: 0845 4747
Visit: nhsdirect.nhs.uk
Round-the-clock service providing immediate and confidential health advice and information, plus dental advice.

Hospitals – Accident & Emergency
With 24-hour casualty departments:
■ Royal Liverpool
Prescot Street L3
Tel: (0151) 706 2000
■ University Hospital Aintree
Lower Lane L9
Tel: (0151) 525 5980
■ Alder Hey Hospital (children only)
Eaton Road L12
Tel: (0151) 228 4811

Walk-In Centres
■ General enquiries
Tel: (0151) 285 3535
Primary Care Trusts, or PCTs, offer treatment and consultations for minor injuries and illnesses with NHS doctors and nurses. Health advice and information is also available on other local services, including out-of-hours doctors, dentists and chemists. No appointment necessary. Mon-Fri 7am-10pm; Sat-Sun 9am-10pm.
■ Liverpool City
Unit 4, Great Charlotte Street L1
■ Old Swan
Crystal Close, St Oswald Street L13

Specialist hospitals
■ Women's Hospital
Crown Street L8
Tel: (0151) 708 9988
Teaching hospital caring for mothers and babies.
■ Dental Hospital
Pembroke Place L3
Tel: (0151) 706 5050
Mon-Fri 8am-5.30pm.

Late-night Chemists
■ Moss Chemists
68/70 London Road L3
Tel: (0151) 709 5271
Daily 8am-11pm.
■ Moss Pharmacy
19 Prescot Road L7
Tel: (0151) 263 2486
Mon-Fri 9.30am-9pm;
Sat 9.30am-8pm.

Helplines

■ Alcoholics Anonymous
Tel: 0845 769 7555
■ Brook Advisory Centre
Tel: (0151) 207 4000
Free confidential advice on birth control for young people.
■ Calm
Tel: 0800 585858
Free and confidential help and advice for young men.
■ Childline
Tel: 0800 1111
■ Merseyside Drugs Council
Tel: (0151) 709 0074
Visit: drugscouncil.com
■ National Drugs Helpline
Tel: 0800 776 600
■ Gamblers Anonymous
Tel: 0161 976 5000
■ Gay Youth R Out
Tel: (0151) 709 6660
Information and support for young people.
■ Mersey AIDS Line
Tel: (0151) 709 9000

■ Office of the Immigration Services Commissioner
Tel: 0845 000 0046
Visit: oisc.gov.uk
Information and advice on regulatory requirements.
■ Pregnancy Advisory Service
Tel: 0161 228 1887
■ Samaritans
Tel: (0151) 708 8888
■ Young Person's Advisory Service
Tel: (0151) 707 1025

Childcare

■ Dukes & Duchesses
Dukes Terrace, Duke Street L1
Tel: (0151) 709 1186
Day nursery with full/part-time places.

Liverpool city council

■ Municipal Buildings
Dale Street L1
Tel: (0151) 233 3000 (general)
Tel: (0151) 233 3001 (environmental)
Tel: (0151) 233 3004 (registrar)
Tel: (0151) 233 3010 (social services)
Visit: liverpool.gov.uk
Mon-Fri 8am-10pm;
Sat-Sun 10am-6pm.

Consulates

■ Consulate of the Cape Verde Republic
20 Stanley Street L1
Tel: (0151) 236 0206
■ Cónsul Honorario de Chile
4 Hardman Street L1
Tel: (0151) 708 6036

■ Consulate of the
Dominican Republic
539 Martins Building, Water Street L2
Tel: (0151) 236 0722
■ Honorary Consulate of Finland
100 Wavertree Boulevard L7
Tel: (0151) 228 8161
■ Consulate of Hungary
43 Rodney Street L1
Tel: (0151) 708 9088
■ Vice Consul of Iceland
Norwich House, Water Street L1
■ Honorary Consulate of Italy
4 Mortimer Street, Birkenhead
Tel: (0151) 666 2886
■ Honorary Consulate
of the Netherlands
Cotton Exchange, Old Hall Street L3
Tel: (0151) 227 5161
■ Royal Consulate of Norway
India Buildings, Water Street L1
Tel: (0151) 236 4871
■ Consulate of Sweden
Port of Liverpool Building,
Pier Head L1
Tel: (0151) 236 6666
■ Royal Thai Consulate
35 Lord Street L2
Tel: (0151) 255 0504

Faith

When 2004 was designated as
Liverpool's Year of Faith there was
increased interest in the churches,
temples and places of worship that
reflect the city's many religious
communities. In the past churches
serving the German, Greek, Italian,
Welsh, Polish and Swedish
populations were established due to
Liverpool's importance as a centre of
shipping, and new arrivals have since
expanded the diversity of faith.

Afro Caribbean
■ Merseyside Caribbean
Community Centre
1 Amberley Street
(near Women's Hospital) L8
Tel: (0151) 708 9790

Buddhism
■ Buddhist Duldzin Centre
25 Aigburth Drive L17
Tel: (0151) 726 8900
■ Kagyu Shedrup Ling Tibetan
Buddhist Centre
15 Hawarden Avenue L17
Tel: (0151) 722 7649

Chinese
■ Chinese Christian Disciples Church
30 Hope Street L1
Tel: (0151) 709 4565
■ Chinese Gospel Church
19-20 Great George Square L1 5DY
Tel: (0151) 709 5050
■ Pagoda Chinese Community Centre
Henry Street L1
Tel: (0151) 708 8833

Christianity
■ Anglican Cathedral
6 Cathedral Close L1
Tel: (0151) 702 7217
■ Diocese of Liverpool
Church House, 1 Hanover Street L1
Tel: (0151) 708 9480
■ Quaker Friends Meeting House
65 Paradise Street L1
Tel: (0151) 708 6361
■ Metropolitan Cathedral
of Christ the King
Mount Pleasant L3
Tel: (0151) 709 9222
■ Roman Catholic Chaplaincy
St Philip Neri Church
Catherine Street L8
Tel: (0151) 709 3858
■ Seventh Day Adventist Church
35 Kensington L7
Tel: (0151) 264 8044

■ Unitarian Church
57 Ullet Road L17 2AA
Tel: (0151) 733 1927

Hinduism
■ Baha'i Centre
1 Langdale Road
(off Smithdown Road) L15
Tel: (0151) 733 8614
■ Hindu Cultural
Organisation
Edge Lane L7 5NA
Tel: (0151) 263 7965

Islam
■ Ar-Rahma Mosque
29-31 Hatherley Street L8
Tel: (0151) 709 7504
■ Liverpool Mosque &
Islamic Institute
8 Cramond Avenue L18
Tel: (0151) 734 1222

Judaism
■ Childwall Hebrew
Congregation
Dunbabin Road L15
Tel: (0151) 722 2979
■ Liverpool Progressive
Synagogue
28 Church Road North L15
Tel: (0151) 733 5871

Sikhism
■ Sikh Gurdwara Temple
Wellington Avenue
Liverpool 15
Tel: (0151) 734 3022

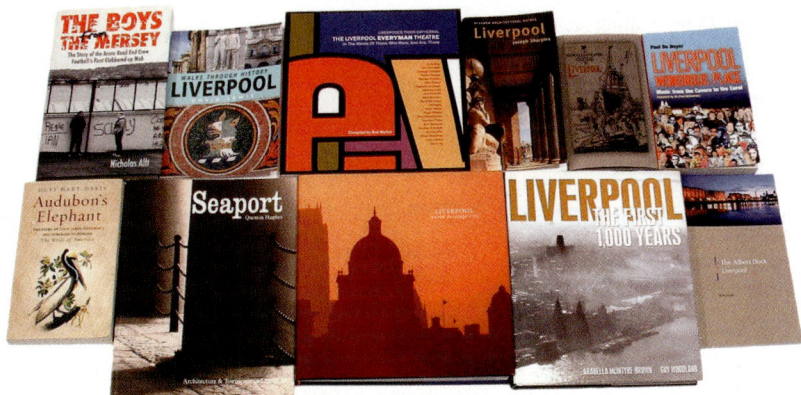

Word up

Some recommended reading...

■ A million pop and football titles, and lots of lavish coffee-table books to choose from, too. Pevsner's new architectural guide to the city, written by Joseph Sharples, is flying of the shelves, while Liverpool: World Heritage City, by Guy Woodland and Lew Baxter, was published to celebrate the UNESCO inscription. Award-winning photographer Woodland also took the evocative pics for Liverpool: The First 1,000 Years, by Arabella McIntyre-Brown – first published in 2001 and the complete history of the city. Check out also Liverpool: City of Architecture, by Professor Quentin Hughes (who also penned Seaport, a seminal account of the city's architecture from 1964); Liverpool: Walks Through History, by David Lewis, a celebration of the beauty and poetry of the urban landscape; The Albert Dock, by Ron Jones, a definitive history with superb photos from then and now; and the recently updated Liverpool: A People's History, by Peter Aughton.

To celebrate its 40th birthday, the Everyman theatre has published a terrific history, 'In the words of those who were, and are, there'. Up at Central Library's Record Office, meanwhile, you can purchase a fascinating facsimile of A Guide to Liverpool 1902, 'with pen and ink sketches', originally published by Littlebury Bros of Crosshall Street.

Another intriguing title is Audubon's Elephant, by Duff Hart-Davis, the story of John James Audubon's epic struggle to publish The Birds of America, starting with his arrival at Liverpool in 1826 (which he recorded vividly in his memoirs).

Musos need look no further than Liverpool Wondrous Place: Music from the Cavern to the Coral, by Paul Du Noyer, the ultimate encyclopaedia of the Scouse sound now out in paperback with a foreword by Sir Paul McCartney. For popular fiction, try Outlaws, by Kevin Sampson, a tense thriller set in South Liverpool and told in the city's vernacular. Brass, by Helen Walsh, is another bare-knuckle urban adventure, while The Boys from the Mersey, by Nicholas Allt, charts the Continental escapades of Liverpool FC's streetwise supporters in the late 70s.

The city has all the major booksellers and some fascinating second-hand stores around the top of Bold Street (Rope Walks) and up towards the University. In Central Library, too, you'll find some real gems among its superb selection on the second floor. Scully, by the legendary Alan Bleasdale,

is a seminal Liverpool classic first published in 1975 and chronicling the adventures of a teenage scallywag.

Look for anthologies by Adrian Henri, Roger McGough and Brian Patten, the poets of the Mersey Sound (the pop movement of the 1960s). And for great bedside reading try the prolific Richard Whittington-Egan, a former Daily Post columnist, and Frank Kane, the king of Liverpool murder and mystery.

Among the classics, you'll find passages about Liverpool in Daniel Defoe's A Tour Through England and Wales, as well as Billy Budd and Redburn by Herman Melville (author of Moby Dick), and more recently Nicholas Monsarrat's The Cruel Sea.

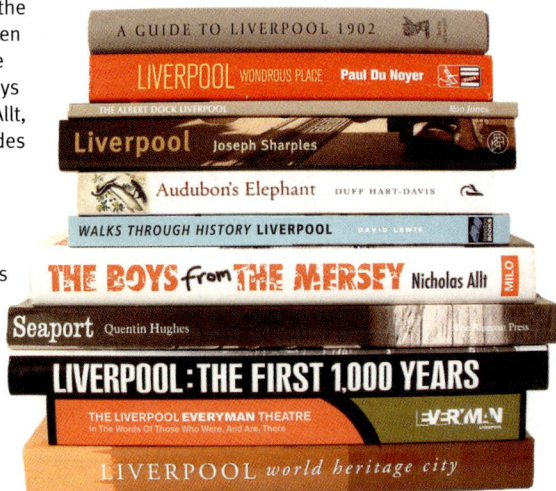

A GUIDE TO LIVERPOOL 1902

LIVERPOOL WONDROUS PLACE Paul Du Noyer

THE ALBERT DOCK LIVERPOOL

Liverpool Joseph Sharples

Audubon's Elephant DUFF HART-DAVIS

WALKS THROUGH HISTORY LIVERPOOL DAVID LEWIS

THE BOYS From THE MERSEY Nicholas Allt MILO

Seaport Quentin Hughes

LIVERPOOL: THE FIRST 1,000 YEARS

THE LIVERPOOL EVERYMAN THEATRE In The Words Of Those Who Were, And Are, There EVERYMAN

LIVERPOOL world heritage city

Walks, tours and cruises

Combination tickets are available for some tours and attractions. Check individually or at the Tourist Information Centres where you can also make bookings. Call Tourist Hotline on 0906 680 6886 for full details (calls cost 25p per minute).

City Centre

■ **The Yellow Duckmarine**
Tel: **(0151) 708 7799**
Visit: **theyellowduckmarine.co.uk**
Hour-long land-and-river tour of waterfront, city and docks, on authentic WWII landing craft. Daily from 11am. £9.95 adult, £7.95 child (two to 15), £29 family, £8.95 concession, registered disabled, carer. Ticket entitles holder to £1 discount on The Beatles Story entrance. Ticket office and pick-up: Albert Dock. No wheelchair access.

■ **City Sightseeing Tour**
Tel: **(0151) 933 2324**
Hour-long open-top bus trip of city-centre with Blue Badge guide. Daily from 11am. £6 adult, £4.50 child (five to 15), £16 family, £4.50 senior citizen. Pick-up: The Beatles Story, Albert Dock. No wheelchair access.

■ **Wingate Tours**
Tel: **(0151) 547 2713**
Explore the city-centre and Beatles sites with a guide. Caters for parties of up to 100 people.

Culture, Heritage & Wildlife

■ **Mersey Ferries River Explorer Cruise**
Tel: **(0151) 630 1030**
Visit: **merseyferries.co.uk**
Fifty-minute cruise on the Mersey for the best views of Liverpool's spectacular waterfront. Stop off at Seacombe Aquarium or Pirates Paradise, a play area for children. Mon-Fri 10am-3pm; Sat-Sun 10am-6pm every hour. £2.30 single/4.50 return adult, £1.30, £2.50 child (five to 15), £11.70 family, £1.80, £3.30 concession. Combined tickets available for cruise and Aquarium Departs: Pier Head.

■ **Special Cruises on the River**
Throughout the year there are themed river trips: Liverbird Wildlife Discovery, Liverpool Bay, Caribbean Evening, Beatles, 1960s, Glam Rock, Halloween and Fireworks and Children's Xmas Cruises. Call above for details and schedule.

■ **Central Library Tour**
Tel: **(0151) 233 5844**
The second floor of the Central Library on William Brown Street has a fine book collection open to the public. Guided tours on second Tuesday of each month from 2.15pm.

■ **Sandon Dock Visitor Centre**
Regent Road, Bootle
Tel: **01925 233 233**
Visit: **nww.co.uk**
Down the plug but where does it go? What actually happens when the water goes down the drain? Come and see inside a wastewater treatment works. Guided tours by appointment. Mon-Fri. Free.

■ **Liverpool Heritage Cab City Tours**
Tel: **(0151) 531 6947**
Experience the city's history in a taxi or 1920s-style car-hire tour.

■ **Radio City Tower**
Tel: **(0151) 709 3285**
Visit: **radiocity.co.uk**
Guided tours around one of the city's most unusual buildings – and unbeatable views. Sat-Sun £5 adult, £2.50 concession. Limited disabled access, lift.

■ **Liverpool Pub Culture Tour**
Tel: **(0151) 928 6691**
or: **07968 528505**
■ **Joseph Williamson Tunnels**
Smithdown Lane L7
Tel: **(0151) 709 6868**
Visit: **williamsontunnels.co.uk**
What lies beneath? A fascinating underground network of tunnels, built in the 19th Century, plus exhibitions depicting the life and times of the eccentric who built them. Apr-Oct: Tue-Sun 10am-5pm. Oct-Mar: Thu-Sun 10am-4pm. £3.50 adult, £2 child, £5 family, £3 concession. Very limited disabled access.

■ **Cains Brewery**
Stanhope Street L8
Tel: **(0151) 709 8734**
Visit: **cainsbeer.com**
Victorian brewery producing award-winning tours including buffet and two pints in Brewery Tap pub. Mon-Thu 6.30pm-8pm. £3.75 over 18s only.

Walks

■ **City Walks**
Tel: **(0151) 652 3692**
Explore the city's architecture and art on foot with a Blue Badge guide. May-Sept. Departs: Tourist Information Centre, Queen Square.

■ **Sunday City Walks**
Tel: **(0151) 928 0630**
Weekly walking tours with Blue Badge guide. Sun 2pm. Departure point: Tourist Information Centre, Queen Square.

Albert Dock & Waterfront Walk
Tel: (0151) 336 1818
Take in the stories and buildings of the historic waterfront on a 90-minute exploration with a qualified guide. Thu-Sat 11.15am & 2pm. £3 adult, £2 under16s and senior citizens. Departs: Gower Street, Albert Dock.

Slavery History Trail
Tel: (0151) 726 0941
Guided tours of areas connected to Liverpool's slave trade. Sat-Sun 11am. £2.50 adult, £1.50 under16s and senior citizens.

Mersey Tourism Blue Badge
Tel: (0151) 237 3925
Over 30 Blue Badge guides available for car, coach and walking tours. Foreign language guides on request, plus 12-seater mini bus hire.
The following guides have specialist knowledge:

Sylvia McMurty
Tel: (0151) 709 9313
or: 0771 500 2464
(Beatles and Liverpool car, coach, minibus and walking tours day and evening).

Hilary Oxlade
Tel: (0151) 931 3075
or: 07803 206 599
(car and minibus tours of Liverpool and Northwest, plus Beatles).

Phil Coppell
Tel: (0151) 920 7568
or: 07710 507 656
(professional guiding service for city, sport, media and Beatles).

Phil Hughes
Tel: (0151) 228 4565
or: 07961 511 223
(German-speaking guide for ale trails and sports tours).

Jerry Williams
Tel: (0151) 608 3769
(Merseyside and the American Civil War).

Beatles tours

The Beatles Story
Britannia Vaults, Albert Dock
Tel: (0151) 709 1963
Visit: beatlesstory.com
Relive the rise of the band from the Cavern to Beatlemania. The complete Fab Four experience.
Daily Apr-Sept 10am-6pm; Oct-Mar 10am-4pm. £7.95 adult, £4.95 child, £23 family, £4.45 concession. Fully accessible.

Magical Mystery Tour
Tel: (0151) 709 3285
or: 0871 222 1963
Visit: cavern-liverpool.co.uk
Two-hour tour starts at the Beatles Story and ends at the Cavern Club on Mathew Street, taking in all Fab Four references along the way. Daily. £10.95. Departs: 2.10pm Queen Square, 2.30pm The Beatles Story, Albert Dock. Extra tours throughout year, call to check.
No wheelchair access.

Cavern City Tours
Specialised Beatles tours and weekend packages, including International Beatles Week in August. No wheelchair access.
Contact as above.

Live@pool Tours
Tel: (0151) 330 0844
Visit: liveapool.com
Themed coach tours. In English, call Jackie Spencer on 07990 761478; Japanese, Shuji Tohyama on 07867 627362

Mendips and 20 Forthlin Road
Tel: (0151) 708 8574 (morning tours)
or: (0151) 427 7231 (afternoon tours)
Visit: spekehall.org.uk
The childhood homes of John Lennon and Paul McCartney respectively. These are National Trust properties, visits are only available with organised tours. 27 Mar-31 Oct, Wed-Sun. £12 National Trust members, £6 non-members, accompanied children free. Departs: 10.30am & 11.20am Albert Dock; 2.15pm & 3.55pm Speke Hall.

Beatles Car Tours
Call to arrange a personalised trip with guide:
Sylvia McMurtry on (0151) 709 9313 and Hilary Oxlade on (0151) 931 3075

Takuji Abe
Tel: (0151) 220 9543
Japanese-speaking Beatles guide.

Other Beatles attractions

Beatles Shop
31 Mathew Street L2
Tel: (0151) 236 8066

Cavern Club
Mathew Street L2
Tel: (0151) 236 1965

Cavern Pub
Mathew Street L2
Tel: (0151) 236 4041
Visit: cavern-liverpool.co.uk

From Me To You
Cavern Walks, Mathew Street L2
Tel: (0151) 227 1963
Visit: beatles64.co.uk

Mathew Street Gallery
Mathew Street L2
Tel: (0151) 236 0009
Exhibition of John Lennon's art and Beatles photos with limited-edition prints for sale.

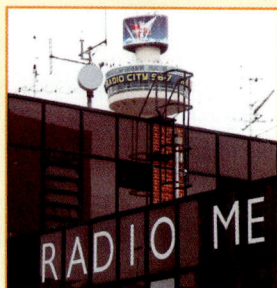

Sport

■ Aintree Racecourse & The Grand National Experience
Ormskirk Road, Aintree L9
Tel: **(0151) 522 2921**
Visit: **aintree.co.uk**
Experience the wonder of the world-famous Grand National steeplechase racecourse and its sumptuous facilities. Includes a trip on the Grand National simulator, tour of the legendary course, stables, weighing room and visit to the mythical Red Rum's grave and Aintree Museum. Twice a day, 22 May-21 Oct.

■ Everton FC Tour
Goodison Park L4
Tel: **(0151) 330 2277**
Visit: **evertonfc.com**
Award-winning tour that lasts for over one hour and can accommodate individuals, small parties and large groups (with optional two-course meal). Mon, Wed and Fri: 11am & 2pm. £6.50 adult, £4.50 children/over 65s, £18 family.
Strictly advance booking.

■ Liverpool FC Museum & Tour Centre
Anfield Road L4
Tel: **(0151) 260 6677**
Visit: **liverpoolfc.tv**
Home of England's most successful football club. Highlights in the museum include four huge European Cups, a 60-seat cinema and re-creation of the famous standing Spion Kop. Don't forget to touch the 'This Is Anfield' sign by the players tunnel. Every weekday 10am-5pm

(hour before kick-off on matchdays). Museum & Tour: £9 adults £9.00, £5.50 children/OAPS, family £23. Museum only: £5 adults £5.00, £3 children/OAPS, £13 families. Strictly advance booking.

TV and radio
■ BBC North West and Granada (part of the ITV network) broadcast regular news bulletins throughout the day on terrestrial TV as well airing a variety of regional programmes. The main radio stations are BBC Radio Merseyside (95.8FM), Radio City 96.7 and 107.6 Juice FM.

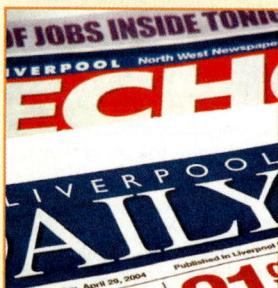

Newspapers and magazines
■ Liverpool Daily Post & Echo
Morning and evening sister newspapers established in the city for the best part of 200 years. The Daily Post has a long history of progressive liberalism, while the Echo is an institution among ordinary Liverpudlians. Published daily, Mondy to Saturday (the Football Echo, published Saturdays during the football season, provides the latest news and action from the region's teams, plus lots of other sport).
■ Space
The city's premier lifestyle magazine. Bi-monthly. Free.
■ Your Move
Property magazine. Fortnightly. Free.
■ Move Out
Listings magazine. Monthly. Free.

■ Live Magazine
Listings for all live performances. Every six weeks. Free.
■ Inform
Bite-sized listings fanzine with good clubbing section. Monthly.
■ Another Late Night
Edgy skate-culture citybeat mag. Bi-monthly. Free.
■ The Evertonian
Official mag of Everton FC. Monthly.
■ LFC Magazine
Official mag of Liverpool FC. Weekly.
■ The Kop
News and gossip for Liverpool FC fanatics. Monthly.

Colleges and universities
■ Blackburne House
Blackburne Place L3
Tel: **(0151) 709 4356**
Visit: **blackburnehouse.co.uk**
Technology centre for women. The historic building dates from 1785.
■ European Languages Centre
43-45 Pembroke Place L3
Tel: **(0151) 708 7071**
Visit: **eurolang.com**
English language school for visitors. Also offers most European languages including Japanese, Turkish, Russian and Chinese dialects.
■ ICDC
Faraday House, Edge Lane L7
Tel: **(0151) 794 2000**
Visit: **icdc.org.uk**
International Centre for Digital Content. New technology, part of JMU.

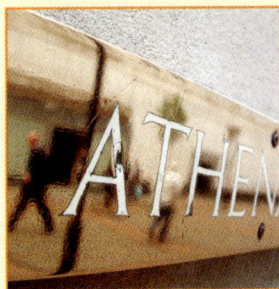

■ **Liverpool Community College**
Tel: **(0151) 252 3000**
Visit: **liv-coll.ac.uk**
Four brand new buildings in the city
centre and courses from performing
arts to travel and tourism to fashion
and clothing.
■ **Liverpool Institute**
of Performing Arts
Mount Street L1
Tel: **(0151) 330 3000**
Visit: **lipa.ac.uk**
LIPA is regarded as one of the
country's outstanding fame
academies. Paul McCartney is the
leading patron, and it's devoted to
providing excellent learning
programmes and resources for
budding actors, dancers, musicians,
technicians, managers and designers.
■ **University of Liverpool**
Tel: **(0151) 794 2000**
Visit: **liv.ac.uk**
One of the UK's leading universities,
renowned for its world-class teaching
and research excellence. Six faculties,
eight Nobel Laureates to date, a grand
total of 54 departments and schools,
nearly 3,000 international students
and over 400 industry partners.
And a splendid campus to match.
■ **Liverpool John Moores University**
Tel: **(0151) 231 2121**
Visit: **livjm.ac.uk**
One of Merseyside's greatest assets,
with an influence stretching far further
than the city boundaries. Boasts
20,000 students and 2,500 staff,
plus exciting new developments like
the Liverpool Science Park on Mount

Pleasant (adjacent to the Metropolitan
Cathedral), encouraging the growth
and development of new knowledge-
based businesses in the area and
nurturing talent within the higher
education sectors.

Clubs and societies
■ **Artists Club**
5 Eberle Street L2
Tel: **(0151) 236 2940**
Opulent surroundings just off Dale
Street, opposite Garlands nightclub
and behind an unassuming blue door.
In existence since 1877 and now
primarily a gentleman's lunching club.
■ **Athenaeum**
Church Alley L3
Tel: **(0151) 709 7770**
A nationally-renowned library, top-
class dining room and meeting room,
housed in an elegant building off
Church Street near Bluecoat
Chambers. The original club was
established way back in 1797 to
provide a meeting place where ideas
and information could be exchanged
(its early proprietors played a major
part in the movement to end slavery).
The number of male and female
'proprietors' (full members) is limited
to 500, with another 500 associate
members who do not reside (or whose
businesses are not located) within 25
miles of the Athenaeum.
■ **Duncan Society**
Dept of Sociology,
University of Liverpool,
Eleanor Rathbone Building,

Bedford Street South L69
Tel: **(0151) 794 2986**
Visit: **duncansociety.org.uk**
Named after the city's pioneering 19th
Century Medical Officer. Conceived to
stimulate debate, discussion and
understanding on contemporary
health issues. Open to all.
■ **Liverpool Yemeni Arabic Club**
167a Lodge Lane L8
Tel: **(0151) 734 0550**
Or LYAC for short, working alongside
Yemeni-speaking people in the city
and those interested in Arabic culture.
■ **Marina & Harbourside Club**
Coburg Wharf, Sefton Street L3
Tel: **(0151) 709 7770**
Visit: **liverpoolmarina.com**
Sailing club with an urban feel and
excellent location overlooking the
River Mersey. Fully licensed with
conference facilities and a great
place for Sunday lunch.
■ **Merseyside Inter-Faith Group**
Tel: **(0151) 733 1541**
Multi-denominational meetings
once a month at different venues
for faith-sharing, learning and
mutual enrichment. Anyone is
welcome to come along.
■ **Racquet Club**
Hargreaves Buildings,
5 Chapel Street L3
Tel: **(0151) 236 6676**
Visit: **raquetclub.co.uk**
Since transformed into an elegant
boutique hotel near the waterfront,
it still plays host to a sporting club
founded back in 1874, with lovely
reception rooms and bars.

Cinemas
■ **Picture House @ FACT**
88 Wood Street L1
Tel: **(0151) 707 4450**
■ **UGC Cinemas**
Edge Lane Retail Park L13
Tel: **0870 155 5146**
■ **Odeon London Road**
London Road L3
Tel: **0870 505 0007**

Site seeing

Where to find Liverpool on the www...

Photography

■ simonjones.co.uk/photography
Local snapper's gallery of Quick Time movies, including 360-degree panoramic views from the Pier Head and the top of the Liver Building.

■ liverpoolphotography.co.uk
Great aerial shots by Simon Kirwan, former Observer Outdoor Photographer of the Year whose images have appeared in many books and magazines.

■ liverpoolphotos.com
Epic skyscapes by Guy Woodland, photographer from Liverpool: The First 1,000 Years (see recommended reading).

■ liverpoolpictorial.co.uk
Fabbest of the fab, categorised by postcode with some wonderful shots of the gritty docklands. Check out those marine dredgers!

Culture and heritage

■ liverpoolculture.com
Official site celebrating the 2008 European Capital of Culture title and reporting on the projects planned for the greatest show on earth.

■ artinliverpool.com
Art gallery listings, weblog, artists details and news. A comprehensive resource for the Liverpool art scene.

■ liverpoolarchitecture.com
Joint-venture by the University and Liverpool Architecture Society, with online tours of the best buildings in the Business District.

■ mersey-gateway.org
A huge project that will eventually incorporate 20,000 digital images illustrating the history and growth of the port of Liverpool.

■ lmu.livjm.ac.uk/etms
Unique database of Liverpool life compiled by John Moores University, with photographs and artefacts from the last eight centuries.

■ liverpoolhistorysociety.org.uk
Online forum for local historians and anyone with a story to tell. They also publish a regular newsletter and annual journal.

■ merseymouth.com
Prose and poetry, whimsy and nostalgia. From the hottest nightclub in 70s Liverpool to the quest for a docker's overcoat.

Regeneration

■ liverpoolvision.com
Excellent site documenting the city's fast-paced renaissance under the so-called Strategic Regeneration Framework produced by Liverpool's public and private sectors.

■ liverpool2007.org.uk
Gateway to the city's historic past plus an insight into the forces that are shaping modern Liverpool in the run-up to its 800th anniversary.

■ liverpoolpsda.co.uk
The official site of the Liverpool Paradise Street Development Area. The whole idea, the big overview, the masterplan, the little details and, ahem, the roadworks.

General information

■ visitliverpool.com
Official tourism site created by The Mersey Partnership. Arts and culture, sport and entertainment, events and attractions.

■ liverpool.gov.uk
The Council's official site. Everything you ever wanted to know about how the city of Liverpool is run, with a comprehensive A-Z section.

■ bbc.co.uk/liverpool
Excellent local coverage from the Beeb with news and listings, a webcam updated every five minutes and lively expats forum.

■ icliverpool.co.uk
Online version of the Liverpool Daily Post & Echo packed with up-to-the-minute information and some handy restaurant reviews.

■ merseyguide.co.uk
'To bring you the information you need to explore and enjoy the county of Merseyside'. Visitors can subscribe to a newsletter.

■ seeliverpool.com
40 pages of information and more than 70 links, with suggested sightseeing schedules and a concise guide for Beatles fans.

Football (unofficial)

■ bluekipper.com
Virulent and vociferous Everton FC fan site, with a great section on funnies overheard at the match. Warning: the language can be choice.

■ raotl.co.uk
Web version of the Liverpool FC fanzine, Red All Over The Land. All the Kopite banter, no shortage of opinion and some cracking T-shirts for sale.

■ shankly.com
Online shrine to the legendary Liverpool FC manager and one of the city's greatest adopted sons. "The problem with you, son, is that your brains are all in your head..."

Index

Get Fresh and Tasty in Merseyside

Advantages of Buying Local Produce

• Consumers are increasingly seeking out local produce because of its finer taste, freshness and clearer traceability.

• Outlets such as farm shops and farmers marekts allow the consumer the opportunity to meet the producer face to face and ask questions.

• Consumers can be more confident about the origins of the food they are buying

• Food is fresher and therefore of a higher nutritional value. On average supermarket food travels 1000 miles compared to the average 30 miles at farmers markets.

• Traditions relating to the production of local food can be preserved.

• Packaging is usually reduced which is better for the environment.

• Rearing, slaughtering and selling animals locally helps to prevent the spread of disease.

• Buying local produce helps the local economy by preserving jobs in the area.

• Buying local produce and supporting companies that buy local produce helps to maintain the countryside.

Merseyside Farmers Markets

Merseyside Farmers Markets offer an ideal opportunity for small producers to sell direct to discerning customers. Most of the produce is specific to the area, and all the producers who sell on the markets are recruited from within a 50-mile radius.

Liverpool - Monument Square - London Road
Next to TJ Hughes,
Contact Rob Lucas, Tel: 0151 233 2165
1st and 3rd Saturday in every month 2005/6

Maghull - Mahull Square
Contact 0151 934 4283 1st Sunday every month 2005/6

Bootle - Next to Bootle library
Contact 0151 934 4283/4159/4285
3rd Thursday every month 2005/6

Southport - King Street, Southport
Contact 0151 934 4283/4159/4285
Last Thursday every month 2005/6

Wirral - New Ferry Village Hall
Grove Street, New Ferry, Wirral Contact 0151 643 1393 2nd Saturday every month 2005/6

Aigburth - Lark Lane - Starts June
Contact Rob Lucas 0151 233 2165

Bark in the Park with Farmers Market - 15th May
Contact Rob Lucas 0151 233 2165

Celebration of Food - 17th July
Contact Rob Lucas 0151 233 2165

To learn more about local and regional produce please contact Suzanne at the Local Food First Project.

Local Food First, c/o North West Fine Foods,
Suite One, West Lancs Technology Management Centre,
Moss Lane View, Skelmersdale, Lancashire, WN8 9TN

Tel: **01695 732734**   Web: **www.nwff.co.uk**

Photography

■ All pictures by David Cottrell except:
Chris Abram (pp32 main, 69, Liver Building
postcard); **Tracy Smith (p204)**; Everyman-
Playhouse (pp17 top, 189, 192); **Liverpool
Daily Post & Echo (pp17 middle left, 40 top
and middle, 57 bottom, 159, 160, 161, 165,
167 top, 179 bottom, 195, 197, 198)**; Joel
Jelen (p17 middle right); **National Museums
Liverpool (pp18, 80 inset, 172, 173 top, 174,
175)**; River City (pp26/27); **Wirral County
Council (pp31 inset, 201 top, 203, 205)**;
Liverpool Vision (p34 bottom); **British
Waterways (p34 top)**; KKA Ltd (p34 middle);
**Liverpool Record Office (pp40 inset bottom,
55 inset top, 76 inset bottom left)**; Palm
House (p50 main); **Liverpool City Council
(p60 inset bottom)**; BCA (p66); **Rumford
Investments (pp70 top and middle)**;
Athenaeum (p81 top); **Grosvenor (p81 inset
bottom)**; 3345 Parr Street (p96 bottom);
Frenson (p97 bottom); Britannia Adelphi
Hotel (p115 inset middle); **60 Hope Street
(p127)**; Piccolino (p139 top); **Baby Cream
(p146 top)**; Garlands (p147 main); **Newz Bar
(p148 main)**; Dave White (p166 inset);
Crush Communications (p167 bottom);
Bluecoat Display Centre (p177 top); **Central
Library (p177 middle)**; Tate Liverpool (p179
top); **LEAP (pp185, 188)**; Liverpool Empire
(pp186, 187); **Southport Jazz Festival
(p193)**; Carling Academy (p194 main).

LIVERPOOL
THE GUIDE 2005/06